LIBRARIES GOT GAME

ALIGNED LEARNING
THROUGH MODERN BOARD GAMES

BRIAN MAYER AND CHRISTOPHER HARRIS

ALLEGHENY COUNTY
LIBRARY ASSOCIATION

AMERICAN LIBRARY ASSO
CHICAGO   2010

D1409942

Brian Mayer is a library technology specialist for Genesee Valley BOCES, an educational services agency that supports the libraries of twenty-two small, rural districts in western New York, as well as an independent library consultant on gaming in libraries. His focus is on modern board games and putting authentic games into educational settings to engage students with the curriculum. He has been instrumental in the growth of designer games as educational resources and has written several documents aligning games with national and state standards. He is the author of many articles on gaming in libraries and writes on the subject in his blog *Library Gamer* (http://librarygamer.wordpress.com). Mayer earned his elementary teaching certification at Buffalo State and his MLS at the University of Buffalo.

Christopher Harris, author of the blog *Infomancy*, is the coordinator of the school library system for Genesee Valley BOCES. In addition to his writing on *Infomancy*, he is a regular technology columnist for *School Library Journal*, talking about "The Next Big Thing." Along with Andy Austin, Harris wrote an ALA TechSource *Library Technology Reports* issue on using the open source Drupal content management framework in libraries, which was published in 2008. He was a participant in the first ALA Emerging Leaders program in 2007 and was honored as a *Library Journal* Mover and Shaker in 2008. An avid gamer, Harris was a member of the ALA/Verizon Foundation Gaming and Literacies grant national panel of experts.

Library of Congress Cataloging-in-Publication Data
Mayer, Brian.
  Libraries got game : aligned learning through modern board games / Brian Mayer and Christopher Harris.
    p. cm.
Includes bibliographical references and index.
ISBN 978-0-8389-1009-2 (alk. paper)
1. Libraries—Special collections—Board games. 2. Board games. 3. School libraries—Activity programs—United States. I. Harris, Christopher, 1977– II. Title.
Z692.B63M39 2010
025.2896—dc22

                                                                                                2009026839

ISBN-13: 978-0-8389-1009-2

Printed in the United States of America
14 13 12 11 10   5 4 3 2 1

This book is dedicated to my wife, without whose infinite patience, support, and understanding it would not have been possible. And to my daughter, who is the reason for everything I do.
—BM

For Christine, with eternal gratitude.
—CH

Contents

 Additional material can be found on the book's website, at
www.ala.org/editions/extras/mayer10092. Look for website material
wherever you see this symbol.

Acknowledgments

Thank you to Genesee Valley BOCES and the member libraries of the region for making the creation of the game library a great success.

To Scott Nicholson for planting the seeds through his incredible knowledge of designer board games and their potential for libraries.

To the American Library Association/Verizon Foundation Gaming and Literacies grant for providing opportunities for sharing in the larger library community.

With appreciation for gamers everywhere whose feedback, input, and suggestions have guided our growth.

PART I
Reintroducing Board Games

Games in libraries are not new, but the idea is undergoing a revival of interest. Developments like the release of the Nintendo Wii as a multigenerational video game console designed for mainstream use have generated a great deal of attention in libraries. The American Library Association responded to this interest with the development of a gaming and literacies grant funded by the Verizon Foundation. Much of the conversation about gaming in libraries has focused on video gaming; that is what most of our students and patrons know. This book will present a different view of gaming, looking at the use of board and card games in school libraries. This is written from the perspective of two school librarians working at a regional school library system. As such, the focus will be on the use of these board and card games as curriculum-aligned instructional resources in libraries and classrooms.

For some schools and libraries, embracing games will present a challenge. Even though so many of our students are gamers, schools can be very reluctant to consider gaming as a part of learning. Given the puritanical need to separate work and play, many adults shy away from being called gamers. It is time to face facts: if you play games, you are a gamer. Welcome to the club.

Designer Games

There is a rich history of board games in American culture. We seem to share fond memories of childhood games like Chutes and Ladders and an overwhelming drive to create a version of Monopoly for every possible theme. Put all of that aside, however, as none of it helps explain the types of games discussed in this book. Here we will talk about modern board and card games either directly descended from or inspired by a wave of European imports. As will be seen, these modern games bear little resemblance to the traditional American style of games involving rolling dice, moving a pawn, and seeing what happens on the square where you land.

There are many names for modern board games. To describe their style (not their place of origin), they are sometimes referred to as Eurogames or European-style board games. This acknowledges the game design renaissance in Germany that led to the recent surge in modern games. These new board games are also called *designer games*. Unlike older games, modern board games usually feature the name of the game designer on the box cover. Just like readers follow authors, gamers will follow game designers who may create games with multiple publishers. Throughout this book, we will use the term *designer games,* which also includes card games that don't use a board. The use of the term also emphasizes the important work of the master game designers who create these excellent resources for school libraries.

WHAT MAKES DESIGNER GAMES DIFFERENT

Think about the rules for the iconic American board games like Chutes and Ladders, Candy Land, Monopoly, Sorry!, or Life. In all of these, the primary mechanic for game play is rolling dice and moving the number of spaces shown on the dice. Based on the square where the player's pawn lands, something happens. This simple mechanic makes for easily learned

3

games but does not provide much in the way of intellectual engagement with the game play. Though there are some financial decisions to be made in Monopoly, all of those decision-making opportunities are established by the rolling of dice. Luck trumps every other mechanic in these games. Though many still include an element of luck, designer games are more often built around a series of shared characteristics.

Information-Rich Environment

While risking everything on a roll of the dice can be exhilarating, it does not offer much in the way of long-term engagement and repeat play value. Recognizing this, modern game designers present a range of options spaced along a continuum defined on either end by chance and strategy.

Examples of these two extremes can be seen in traditional games like war and chess. In the first, players randomly compare two cards from dealt decks; there is no opportunity for strategy, as the cards are randomly distributed and randomly drawn for comparison. On the other hand, chess is what is called a perfect information game. Both players have access to the same information about the current state of the game and all potential moves are known at all times. Games of pure chance can grow boring because there is no opportunity for improvement, while improvement in games of pure strategy can require a huge commitment to studying and mastering the actions and reactions found in established styles of play. There are passionate supporters of both extremes, but most casual game players are looking for something in the middle.

There are designer games available to accommodate many different levels of chance and strategy across a wide variety of genres. For example, players can choose between two racing games, Formula D and Bolide, for a game that meets their preferred style. In Formula D, players make strategic decisions as they shift up and down through gears to navigate the track. Movement of each player's car token is determined through the roll of a die for each gear; third gear, for example, is represented by an eight-sided die with the sides showing four, five, six, six, seven, seven, eight, and eight. This means that statistically you are much more likely to move six, seven, or eight spaces than the minimum of four, but the strong element of chance means a roll of four can lead to a drastic loss of position on the track. In comparison, Bolide provides a near-perfect information environment where players use vector movement rules to select each move. Instead of rolling dice, players use a momentum marker to determine their range of possible moves based on their current vector of motion. A car can be pushed as fast as desired, but a player's understanding of physics and Newton's laws will quickly be revealed as cars drift into corners with too much sideways momentum. Chance only enters the game in a few situations such as dice rolls to determine a fast, normal, or slow start or to resolve possible collisions between two cars. It is also important to note that the use of chance in these situations is a natural manifestation of the theme. Tires catch during a start, or a driver may execute a last-minute steering maneuver to narrowly avoid a crash. Rolling dice creates excitement that matches the theme without overwhelming the need for skill.

For schools and libraries, the continuum defined by chance and strategy probably has the most impact on how the game approaches the use of information. If Formula D had players roll simple six-sided dice with an equal chance for each number one through six, then there would be no need to process any information as the outcome would be decided purely by chance. Compared to mainstream American games, Formula D introduces a higher level of information processing by requiring statistical analysis to select a gear with a certain die roll range. Bolide demands a high level of information processing as players must constantly plan ahead for speed increases and decreases to address shifting vectors of momentum. Another way to look at these differences is to consider the role of chance in these games as a stand-in for knowledge. Instead of chance, Bolide requires an advanced understanding of physics, while Formula D uses the chance roll of a die instead of vector calculations. Therefore, the chance/strategy continuum in many cases can also be seen as a complexity continuum that defines the level of background knowledge and information processing required by a game.

Open-Ended Decisions

Another characteristic that is especially prominent in designer games with a strong use of strategy is complex decision making. Along with a high level of information, many games present players with a more open-ended play environment. Each turn in Puerto Rico, players select the role they want to take as they develop plantations and other buildings on their island. As with Bolide, Puerto Rico is a perfect information game dominated by strategy; the only thing left to chance is selecting the types of plantation crops available for development each round. Unlike the singular method of winning found in Bolide, however, Puerto Rico presents a rich selection of opportunities for success. As with real-world markets, some players in Puerto Rico will profit by growing and selling crops, while others will focus on building valuable real estate. The large number of possible building combinations, along with imposed scarcity for each building type, forces players to be flexible. Successful strategies have emerged, but players can experiment with new ways of interacting with the game and with new strategies.

As will be seen later, the open nature of many designer games is one of the characteristics that makes them especially powerful in schools and libraries. When players are making complex decisions, they have to process more information and use higher-order thinking skills. This use of information literacy skills is the foundation upon which game/curriculum alignments can be developed. Puerto Rico forces players to investigate a constantly shifting game environment, use an inquiry-like process of considering options, and evaluate both their game play and the play of others. Contrast this to the decision making and information processing in a game like Monopoly, where rolling dice and moving a pawn leads to one of the few decisions in the game: to buy the property or not.

End-Game Scoring

Many designer games are created to engage players in a shared community of play that allows for ongoing development. In most cases, these games are not a race to eliminate players so that the last player surviving can be named the winner, as is found in so many traditional American games. Instead, designer games tend to feature end-game scoring based on victory points gained through the completion of goals or gathering of resources. This means that players can be part of the game play throughout the game, as opposed to being forced to withdraw from the experience to sit as spectators on the sidelines. In a school or library setting, those players who were eliminated early present a challenge: Will their being removed from the game create a disruption when they are left with nothing to do?

Ticket to Ride is a train game often used as a gateway game—an accessible game that serves as an introduction to designer games. In this game, players work to build train routes across America that connect cities and meet individual goals. Throughout the game, points are scored on a track around the edge of the board—an increasingly common feature in many designer games—but the real victor may not emerge until the hidden objective cards are revealed at the end of the game. Even if a player feels she might not be in the running to win, she can still have a huge impact on the outcome of the game by completing critical train routes to block other players. Unlike elimination-style games, designer games that use an end-of-game scoring mechanic like this can keep everyone engaged, reducing the potential for disruptions from disengaged (and perhaps even disheartened) participants, and also facilitating moving groups through a series of games as a cohesive unit.

Balancing the Theme

The most complex feature of many designer games is an intricate interplay between mechanics and theme. There are a number of common game mechanics—the process by which game play proceeds—found in designer games. Designers often use theme (the setting, characters, and general concept behind a game that establish a purpose for playing) to create a unique game that extends the mechanics to new levels. Some games achieve a harmonious balance of mechanics and theme, but often there is one attribute that is more dominant. This does not diminish the game in any way and is actually the source of many strong alignments to content area standards.

At first glance, Oregon is a game that offers a very strong westward expansion theme. Players establish communities in Oregon by taking turns placing building tiles and people in groups on the board. The thematic links to a social studies curriculum are, however, tenuous at best. There is no in-depth consideration of why people are moving to Oregon or why communities form where they do. Oregon, it turns out, is a math game. Tiles are placed on the board by collecting sets of cards that match symbols along the sides of the board. By playing two cards, players define a pair of Cartesian coordinates where tiles can be placed. This mechanic is certainly not the primary selling point of the game from the publisher's standpoint, though it does make the game well suited for use in schools and libraries.

Even though Oregon may not be selected for use in a school library on account of its theme, that theme is still a critical part of the game. The theme creates a context for play that helps explain the rules. One of the more powerful building tiles in the game is the train station; playing this tile is naturally limited to map spaces that have train tracks. By providing thematic support for rules or play mechanics, designers invite players further into the experience of playing the game. This immersion is what makes games such a powerful tool for learning. Unlike a so-called educational game that might have been designed to teach Cartesian coordinates, Oregon was designed for strong play value within a richly themed environment that just happens to use Cartesian coordinate mapping as a mechanic.

Game Mechanics

Given the complexity of many designer games, it helps that they often make use of common mechanics; this makes it easier for players to learn new games. Schools and libraries can use this as a scaffold to prepare students for more complex games.

Roll-and-Move. Though certainly not as common a mechanic as in traditional American board games, there are still designer games that use dice to control movement. The difference is that the designer games often give players a higher level of control over either the dice being rolled or what happens as a result of the roll. Based on the results on two regular six-sided dice, players in Enchanted Forest can move in any direction in any combination of the two results (four forward, complete an action, five backward, for example).

Open Movement. Some games remove the dice completely in favor of movement points or action points that may be used to move or complete other actions. This gives the player a much higher level of control over his character in the game. This point is illustrated by comparing two different dungeon-crawling role-playing games: The traditional American game Talisman has players roll a die, trying to get the one number needed to land on the spot that allows them to move forward in the game. Such a high level of chance introduces a great deal of frustration as players bounce back and forth around the one spot they need to hit. In contrast, Prophecy is a designer game that uses open movement to give players control over the game. Players can move one space in either direction for free, pay coins for a horse to move two spaces, pay a few more coins to take a ship from one port to another, or even use coins to travel through portals.

Worker Placement. Another common mechanic found in designer games is worker placement. For example, in Stone Age, a worker placement game that uses a strong element of chance to re-create the struggles of an early tribe to gather resources and thrive, players are not moving around a board. Instead, players are placing pawns into certain areas on the board to receive benefits during a resolution phase, thus the concept of worker placement. In this case, small wooden figures representing the members of a Stone Age tribe can be assigned to various gathering tasks that can result in food or other resources.

This style of game tends to focus on resource management. Not only must players plan ahead to receive maximum benefit from their limited supply of workers, but in most cases those workers are also producing goods that will be applied in various combinations for victory points. Stone Age's workers gather resources that can be turned in for special victory cards. At the same time, however, some workers will always need to be tasked with gathering the food required to sustain the tribe each turn. In addition to resource management, worker placement games also tend to feature higher requirements for time management. There are many more things in Stone Age that you will want (or even need!) to do than can be done in either a turn or the whole game. The placement of every worker ends up being more precious than expected.

Simultaneous Action. RoboRally is a chaotically fun game that teaches rudimentary programming as up to seven players simultaneously move their robots around the board. Games that use this mechanic are great for large groups, as it minimizes the downtime that comes with a player waiting for her next turn. In order to work, this mechanic also often requires a higher level of conversation between players. Not all games with this mechanic go to the extreme of RoboRally. Many designer games use some aspect of this by involving players in actions, reactions, and decisions during other players' turns.

Role Selection. One way that some games implement simultaneous action is through the selection and resolution of roles. San Juan, a card game based on Puerto Rico, has players select roles in order to build, produce, or sell goods. Each round, every player has a chance to select a role from the available roles. All the players get to use that role, but the player who selected the role gets a bonus ability. This keeps everyone involved in simultaneous action but provides a more structured environment. The simplicity of San Juan also makes it a great scaffolding game to prepare students for the much more complex Puerto Rico.

Games that use role selection can be more open-ended in their play style. Despite the openness, or perhaps because of it, in many games using this mechanic there will often be a mathematically best choice of role for each player in a round to take. Just as in the almost scripted play of very high-level chess, there can be a game choice that will maximize profit and opportunities for victory while minimizing benefits for other players. Mixing players of different skill levels for role selection games is a potential source of problems. More experienced players can become frustrated as new players make less-than-optimal choices of role.

Cooperative Play. One way to accommodate players with different skill levels is to create a more casual, less competitive play environment using games that feature cooperative play. In this style of game, players are working together as a team against the game itself. Cooperative games range from very simple games for three-year-olds up to games that will provide a strong challenge for the most veteran players. This mechanic demands conversation, so don't plan to use cooperative games in a quiet space. On the other hand, the forced communication makes these games a great resource for speech therapy or English-language-learning classes. Depending on the desired outcome or group dynamics, it is important to note that there are two main subgroups of cooperative games: true cooperatives and traitor-based games.

As a true cooperative game for very young children, Max helps preschool-age children learn to work together toward a common goal. Players take turns rolling two dice with green and black dots on them. For each green dot rolled, that player moves one of the woodland creatures in the game closer to safety; for each black dot rolled, Max the cat creeps closer to the small creatures. The group needs to talk about which animal is the best to move, as they are all working together to control all of the animals. Sometimes, when the creatures are in immediate danger, players will need to not roll and instead use their turn to call Max back to the house for a treat. This can be a hard sacrifice for a very young child to make in that they are giving up their turn for the good of all.

To see the real power of cooperative games, try playing Max as a competitive game where three players are each controlling one of the creatures. The conversation around the board immediately changes and a much darker tone sets in. Players are unwilling to sacrifice a turn to call Max back to save a competitor and so animals that lag behind due to bad dice rolls can quickly be eliminated.

Traitor-based cooperative games introduce some elements of competition while also maintaining the group play aspect of the cooperative mechanic. In some games, there is a chance that one or more players might be a traitor, while other games are designed so that at least one player in the group will definitely be a traitor. Battlestar Galactica ensures that someone will be a traitor, but that person may not find out that he is the traitor until halfway through the game. The inclusion of a traitor makes this already complex and engaging cooperative game even more compelling. The tension of working within a team knowing that someone is (or at least will be) a traitor can be quite appealing. It must be understood, however, that the traitor mechanic can reduce otherwise cooperative games into paranoid grabs for power as players struggle to trust anyone besides themselves. As this is a temporary game environment, the potential for interpersonal conflict is not necessarily something that removes a game from consideration. Simply be aware that not all cooperative games are as focused on team building; games with traitors can include a period of suspicion until the traitors are identified and the team can begin working toward a common goal.

GAMES FOR ALL

Designer games provide rich and engaging play experiences that easily match the level of complexity found in video games. With a variety of mechanics going well beyond the traditional roll-and-move, designer games force players to explore, inquire, interpret, and act upon information gathered from many sources. Perhaps more important for schools and libraries, these games provide a more social environment where players are interacting or collaborating as they play. As will be seen later in this book, many of the games can be aligned with library and information literacy skills and state content standards. Through a combination of game mechanics that reinforce skills and themes that provide context for learning about content, designer games are a valuable resource libraries can provide to support instruction. The introduction of games into schools, however, demands a higher burden of proof to overcome the misconception that playing and learning are separate and distinct states of being.

Why Games Matter

Whether the topic is animal instincts or advanced military training simulations, many learning experiences are built around the idea of fun. So why have most schools been reluctant to embrace play as an instructional method? Children, it often seems, are born with an innate sense of play as a way to explore the word around them, and yet the traditional school day is designed with clear separations between instruction and recreation. Learning in this puritanical context is hard work and therefore must not be diluted with something as trivial as play. Games are seen as the reward for finishing required work, never part of the actual work. In the current educational landscape, where teachers and students alike are overwhelmed by high-stakes testing, how can a school be expected to find more time for play?

The answer is not to make extra time for play, but rather to use the inherent learning potential of game play as a part of the regular instructional program. In much the same way that fiction is used as a way to explore the English language or to provide a context for historical studies, games can be used to extend and enrich many subjects. This is not a radical new idea; there have been many attempts to provide educational games designed to enhance instruction. Unfortunately, most of those resources were not crafted by designers with experience in creating authentic game experiences, and so many fail to capture the essence of play. Yet, with a rich variety of game mechanics to provide skills practice and the opportunity to explore new ideas through thematic elements, many designer games already provide a strong foundation for learning. The school library, already adept at finding connections between curricular and recreational resources in other formats, is the ideal place to reintroduce play as a form of learning using curriculum-aligned designer games.

Advocates for play are often discouraged by attempts to link play and instruction. As David Elkind noted in a recent article entitled "The Power of Play,"

School administrators and teachers—frequently backed by goal-oriented politicians and parents—broadcast the not-so-subtle message that these days play seems superfluous, that at bottom play is for slackers, that if kids must play, they should at least learn something while they are doing it.[1]

While the need for unstructured play is clearly evident, the current educational climate makes a push for free play more of a challenge. By using designer games that can also be aligned to curriculum standards, school libraries can still provide a high quality of play while also remaining focused on student achievement. Like so many other resources in libraries, games enrich and extend classroom instruction while promoting personal and aesthetic growth. In other words, students can (and should) play, but for school libraries to be allowed to support this need it may be necessary to directly attach play to learning.

Designer games can be described as supporting learning in four fundamental ways. Perhaps most important for school libraries is that these games provide an authentic experience for students. Secondly, by collecting and using designer games that are focused on quality game play, libraries are using materials that engage students on a familiar level. Designer games can also reinforce critical social and life skills in an increasingly digital world. Finally, these games align with our core mission of promoting information literacy.

AUTHENTIC EXPERIENCES

One of the commonly noted features of the gaming generation now in our schools (including students and young teachers) is the high level of perceived expertise they have gained through gaming. For example, those who play the computer game Civilization IV get to have the experience of leading a civilization as it grows and develops. They select the technological path to take, shape growth of borders, and choose between diplomacy and war. John Beck and Mitchell Wade explore this further in *Got Game: How the Gamer Generation Is Reshaping Business Forever*:

> Gamers have amassed thousands of hours of rapidly analyzing new situations, interacting with characters they don't really know, and solving problems quickly and independently. Admittedly, they have gained that experience in a simplified world focused almost entirely on themselves. But that world has also emphasized tangible results and given them constant, critical feedback.[2]

The goal of simulation games like Civilization is to present an authentic experience that creates a manageable replica of a situation. Though video games can use graphics to create a more immersive environment, many designer games present equally complex and authentic experiences.

Agricola is a board game that provides a simulation of life for a family of farmers in the seventeenth century. Though not as all-encompassing as the Civilization video game, Agricola provides a complex look at one part of historical life. With a high priority on authenticity, the game forces players to make difficult decisions about what to do with a very limited number of actions. Players start the game with two family members and therefore get two actions each turn. Planning for the future is helpful but not always possible, given the more immediate challenge of feeding a family by the harvest phase at the end of each round. By using a very open-ended worker placement mechanic, the game provides an opportunity for players to develop a level of expertise about being part of a family. There are probably so-called educational games meant to teach players how to work within a family, but without being didactic Agricola presents a play-oriented environment that accomplishes the same task. Just because the game is fun does not mean that it presents any less of an authentic experience. Players will still struggle with the decision to have children; this provides more workers (and an additional daily action) but also requires more food at each harvest.

The authenticity of the experiences presented in a true gaming environment, as opposed to a direct instructional resource masquerading as a game, is derived from the integrated skills found in game play. When players are immersed in the created world of game play, they are surrendering themselves to the modified world rules for the game. In order to be successful at the game, they will have to abide by the rules and make use of the required skills within the game's context. Activities that would be met with disdain within the context of homework are gladly completed within a game.

Designer games often use rich thematic elements to create this context for skill use. Incan Gold has a group of players descending into the ruins of an ancient Incan temple searching for treasure. With each flip of a card, the group of explorers enters a new room. They might find danger, or they might find treasure. Treasure is always welcome but must be shared equally among the group; this may be a band of tomb robbers, but they want to make sure they are being fair. If, for example, a group of five players enters a room that offers fourteen treasures, the loot must be divided as evenly as possible, with the remainder of the treasure pieces placed on the card to be left behind in the room. This is a simple game mechanic, but one that requires students to engage in division with remainders. The key difference between this and a worksheet on division with remainders, however, is the context. In the case of Incan Gold, players have willingly entered into the shared context of exploration created by the game's theme. Within that environment, doing division with remainders is simply a natural activity and not a chore.

STUDENT ENGAGEMENT

Your students are gamers. At least, this is true for the 97 percent of them who play video games, as reported by a Pew Internet and American Life study on "Teens, Video Games, and Civics."[3] This represents a significant enough percentage of the school population that this book is going to unapologetically ignore the 3 percent who do not play games. Even though this statistic refers to video games, the difference is simply one of an electronic format as opposed to an analog format. Games are one of the few activities that cross generation gaps to link teachers with students. At first glance, the latest first-person-shooter or sports video game may not seem to hold up in comparison to the lighter puzzle and card games with which adults may be more familiar, but the experience is the same. No matter the type of game, there is a shared element of play that transcends format, genre, or difficulty. A quick game of solitaire or Bejeweled can provide the same engagement as a marathon session in World of Warcraft. Hard-core gamers may try to dispute this comparison with arguments that success in World of Warcraft takes hours of preparation, months of skill building, and complex interactions with dozens of other players, but they would be missing the point. For some, hours of engagement are both possible and enjoyable. For others, fifteen minutes may be the limit of possibility—but the shorter time span does not mean diminished enjoyment or engagement with the task.

Given this strong shared connection and the near ubiquity of gaming in the lives of our students, how can schools and libraries *not* harness the power of games for instruction? Anyone who has lost track of time while engrossed in a game is familiar with the potential for engagement that play offers. By providing time for game play within the school day, school libraries are really providing students with an opportunity for refreshment through play. The basic idea is not new to libraries; we have long provided interludes through magazines, newspapers, fiction, and other print sources collected for recreational reading. Other libraries provide a chance to unwind with puzzles, and a higher number than you might imagine have had traditional games like chess or checkers available. The medium was never as important as the need that libraries met by providing a place for students (and staff!) to step out of the intensity of the learning environment for a chance to recharge. By using designer games aligned to curriculum standards that provide a combination of authentic play and embedded learning, however, it is possible for school libraries to provide renewal within the learning environment itself.

The real challenge to success in a school library program like this is not gaining support from administrators or other teachers who struggle with the work versus play issue, but rather the difficulty of finding appropriate games that offer the magical blend of engagement and enrichment. Fake games designed to teach will fail to provide the level of engagement demanded by students used to the overwhelming stimulation of video games. Guitar Hero, though quite engaging, struggles to pass the test of games that provide a learning experience. Some designer games, however, manage to blend complex mechanics and rich themes into a game that can work and play well in a school library.

So what type of game fits the bill? My Word! is a quick game from the company behind the incredibly successful Apples to Apples party game. Two to as many students as can fit around a table race to find words as letter cards are flipped by a dealer. Be warned, this is a very fun game that can lead to a bit of exuberant noise. For a similar, though more quiet game, check out Quiddler for another word creation game using letter cards. Like many other designer games, these two examples provide the necessary escape into the familiar and engaging world created by shared game experiences. They do this while also reinforcing English language skills and building vocabulary as students are forced to review a mental list of known words. These games are work, but they are also very much play.

SOCIAL AND LIFE SKILLS

Beyond the dichotomy that values work and demeans play, the other pervasive myths that surround gaming tend to be of a more social nature. The idea of a socially inept group of outcasts huddled in a basement around Dungeons and Dragons rule books, or the equally flawed view of antisocial violent youth going on rampages after being desensitized to violence in Halo, persists in mainstream views of gaming. In reality, a great deal of play is built around intricate social patterns and rules that the whole community of play must support and follow. In *The Genesis of Animal Play,* Gordon Burghardt compiled a list of common types of play in children.[4] Except for the most basic types of physical play or noninteractive parallel play, all of the styles of play require social interaction. The shared fantasy of sociodramatic play relies on participants maintaining their roles within a shared social context; even rough-and-tumble play has a set of shared social rules.

Games, as a structured and rule-oriented form of play, can demand even higher levels of social interaction. Designer games can be especially effective at creating a social experience through the use of complex mechanics. Speech therapists often use games to create a relaxed atmosphere where students can concentrate on an engaging activity while they work on their speech. Cooperative games like Max for very young children or Shadows over Camelot work well for this. Students are not only engaged in play, but these two cooperative games naturally require a high level of communication and information sharing as players work together against the game. Shadows over Camelot, more appropriate for middle or high school students, is an especially challenging game that re-creates the struggles of King Arthur and the knights of Camelot. The game is very attractive, with colorful boards, knight figurines, and many other pieces. When students from different social groups sit down together to play this game, however, they must find common ground in order to be successful. As sports teams need to rise above petty problems to achieve as a team, players in cooperative games must also develop a quick synergy to beat the game.

Max teaches very young children to learn important social skills like working for the good of a group, taking turns, and talking about decisions; Shadows over Camelot teaches about the need for cooperative planning, long-term group strategy, and constant communication. These skills will serve students well not only in classroom projects, but also in future employment when they need to work as part of a team with people they do not select and may not particularly like. While these skills can be found in other types of games, designer games are unique in their ability to gather players around a common board for face-to-face play that is so critical for social development. The shared game experience around the table creates a temporary community of players bound together by the game. Within that group, students have an authentic opportunity to practice social and life skills as they work through game challenges.

HIGHER-ORDER THINKING

Designer games provide another way that school libraries can reinforce the need for inquiry, strategic analysis, problem solving, and critical thinking. As will be explored at length in the next section, there are many games available that address these concepts as seen through alignment with library and information literacy skills.

There is nothing modern about the use of games and play for higher-order thinking. Writing in 1893 on child development, William Preyer noted the importance of play for developing critical thinking in young children:

> We easily overlook in like manner the great intellectual strain connected with the early play of children. How much there is of combination—i.e., of putting together! How much of analyzing or taking to pieces of tangible things! How much of construction and destruction! How much investigation, persistent penetration accompanied with great muscular effort,

into the interior of things that are shut up! The passion for unveiling the veiled, for getting at the concealed, for finding the reason why things hold together, the cause of a noise, the cause of an effect of light—in a word, the insatiable, hereditary appetite for causality in man—this it is which finds its first satisfaction in childish play. Hence come feelings of pleasure, and the removal of the discomfort occasioned by ignorance.[5]

Mainstream American board games tend to be built around closed systems that have players moving around a track completing preset goals. To put this in an educational perspective, the roll-and-move mechanic can be compared to the knowledge or comprehension levels on Bloom's Taxonomy of Educational Objectives. (See table 2.1.)

    With movement and action predetermined by the roll of dice and spaces on the board, there is little or no need for players to move beyond basic levels of thought. For example, in Trivial Pursuit, players move around the board attempting to recall memorized knowledge. In Monopoly, there is some need to comprehend property values and select appropriate matches for current property owned, but these choices are still severely limited by random rolls of the dice. It must be stressed, though, that Bloom's Taxonomy represents a continuum of possible educational objectives and not a hierarchy. The knowledge and comprehension levels are not lower or worse than others; they are just more simplistic in that they require less

TABLE 2.1
Gaming by Bloom's Taxonomy

Bloom's Taxonomy	Skills	Games
Evaluation	argue, assess, compare, judge, predict, support	Chicago Express, Battlestar Galactica, Max
Synthesis	arrange, collect, create, develop, manage, organize, plan	Puerto Rico, Once upon a Time, 1960: The Making of the President
Analysis	appraise, calculate, criticize, examine, question	Bolide, Citadels, Shadows over Camelot
Application	choose, illustrate, dramatize, solve, use	Charades, Portrayal, Numbers League
Comprehension	classify, explain, locate, recognize, select	Pictureka, Monopoly, Lost Cities
Knowledge	memorize, define, arrange, list	Trivial Pursuit, Sorry!, 10 Days in the USA

independent interpretation. There are some wonderful designer games in these levels as well: 10 Days in the USA has players arrange states into a ten-day journey based on a few simple rules for travel. This is not a complicated game, but it does provide a more open mechanic than roll-and-move games and is certainly more curriculum aligned. This does not make it a bad game (it is a great game for upper elementary or middle school social studies), but it would not be the best choice for focusing on higher-order thinking skills.

When the goal is to support higher-order thinking, the designer games dominating the other levels of Bloom's Taxonomy are excellent resources. Once upon a Time is a storytelling card game that requires synthesis of information for an on-the-fly creation of a fairy tale. Players are dealt hands of cards with common objects, ideas, or characters from fairy tales such as an axe, love, sisters, or an evil spell. Using the cards, the first player begins telling a story. As elements from the cards show up, he plays the cards down, attempting to get rid of all the cards he has. The other players are listening for mention of cards that they have or waiting to challenge the incidental use of a card that did not fit into the story. This means that the nonstorytelling players must be functioning at the evaluation level of Bloom's Taxonomy as they look for chances to steal control of the story.

Other games at these levels of Bloom's Taxonomy focus on inquiry and problem solving within a constantly changing game environment. In 1960: The Making of the President, players take on the role of either John F. Kennedy or Richard Nixon during their historic 1960 campaigns. Each side has to develop a strategy for drawing attention to event cards that benefit their candidate while burying those that would prove damaging. There is never enough time to do everything that is necessary; between campaigning in states, keeping up pressure on the issues, making media appearances, and more, players constantly feel they are falling behind. Long-term planning and strategic analysis are the secrets to victory. Players have to remember that the key to winning is having the most electoral votes at the end of game. This means that in early rounds it is critical that players are assessing both the short- and long-term impact of their actions. In other words, this is an entire unit worth of higher-order thinking skills wrapped up in an engrossing game that provides a school librarian with a powerful incentive for collaboration with a high school social studies class.

GAMES DO MATTER

Schools today are searching for ways to address twenty-first-century learning skills with a focus on rigor and relevance. Designer games are a powerful resource school libraries can provide to support this goal. Their complex mechanics and rich themes can provide an authentic and relevant learning experience. By using play, these games engage students in an activity with which they are already very familiar. The play environment also allows the introduction of a much higher level of rigor; given the engagement, students will more willingly rise to the challenge to maintain involvement in the play experience. That shared play experience also creates a localized community where students have to practice positive social and life skills to work together within a game. Finally, many designer games address players at the most complex levels of Bloom's Taxonomy and so require many of the twenty-first-century learning skills that are needed for success. For these reasons, designer games should be added to all school libraries as a new type of instructional resource. In some cases, this might be easier said than done.

Notes

1. David Elkind, "The Power of Play," *American Journal of Play* 1 (Summer 2008): 1.
2. John Beck and Mitchell Wade, *Got Game: How the Gamer Generation Is Reshaping Business Forever* (Boston: Harvard Business School Press, 2004), 80.
3. Amanda Lenhart et al., "Teens, Video Games, and Civics," 2008, www.pew internet.org/Reports/2008/Teens-Video-Games-and-Civics.aspx.
4. Gordon Burghardt, *The Genesis of Animal Play* (Boston: MIT Press, 2006), 97.
5. William Preyer, *Mental Development in the Child* (New York: D. Appleton and Co., 1893), 43.

Redefining Resources

Ask someone what comes to mind when she thinks of libraries, and chances are good she will tell you that she thinks about books. To be more precise, according to an Online Computer Library Center report, there is a 69 percent chance that the primary association for libraries is books.[1] This is hardly surprising, given the numerous shelves holding thousands of books that take up so much space in most libraries. Yet to say that libraries are about books neglects a long history of libraries providing rich collections of nonbook materials. The Northern Liberty Library in Iowa offers a collection of cake pans, the Hastings Public Library in Nebraska loans quilting stencils, and it is relatively easy to find a library that loans artwork or toys for use by patrons. Now it is becoming more common to find libraries that also offer games as part of their collections.

Dr. Scott Nicholson from the Library Game Lab at the Syracuse University School of Information conducted a survey of public libraries in 2007 to gather baseline data about gaming in libraries. At that time, over 70 percent of surveyed libraries reported that they supported gaming, whether through gaming programs, game collections, or allowing gaming in the library. Though over 40 percent of the respondents had formal gaming programs, only about 20 percent loaned games. For those with circulating collections, however, board or card games were the most commonly loaned type of game and were offered by 39 percent of the libraries.[2]

FACING QUESTIONS ABOUT GAMES

With an established foundation for the practice of collecting and loaning games in public libraries, the real question then becomes whether or not games are an appropriate resource for school libraries. At a very simple level, one mission of the school library is to provide a collection of resources for use by the students and staff of the school. Those resources are selected to meet two needs: instructional utility and personal fulfillment. As will be explored further in part 2, designer games can fill both of these collection requirements. To briefly explain this through a more familiar lens, games are evaluated for purchase much like books. Like any good nonfiction book that engages readers while also providing information to support learning, designer games can be selected specifically for their ability to provide both entertainment and curriculum support. Other libraries might be more focused on developing a fiction-type collection of games that places a premium on the enjoyment aspect of the game, but school libraries might find it more important to build a collection of games that can be presented as another format of curriculum-aligned instructional resources.

During the collection development process, games must be addressed like any other type of resource your library might consider. Selection criteria must be clearly established and followed to ensure that a game collection can be defended in the face of possible opposition. In many ways, the creation of a game library can be approached in much the same way that many libraries introduced graphic novels to their collections. In the beginning, each potential purchase must be carefully considered to make sure that it will not overburden a fledgling program with controversy. This isn't to say that games like Dungeons and Dragons don't have a place in school libraries, but the genre in general and this game in particular come with some rather extensive baggage. By focusing on the curriculum alignments and instructional potential of games, it is easier to cast them in a more positive light. As more graphic novels were purchased that did not cause parent outcry, libraries were able to further the perceptual shift. Over time, graphic novels changed from a suspect fringe genre into an accepted format that spanned genres and subject areas.

As with graphic novels, the real challenge for building a game collection is educating teachers, administrators, and parents about the wide range of offerings within a format. Some titles invoke concern, but this cannot condemn the entire range of offerings. In some ways, this makes designer games a great place to start. Most people have fond memories of time spent playing board games as a child; board games are associated with family game nights and time shared with loved ones. With no ill will toward video games, it must be acknowledged that console-based series like Halo and Grand Theft Auto have received a great deal of negative attention. When the games included in this book are presented in schools, they are most often received with blank (though interested) stares. This lack of prior knowledge means the first impression of the games can be carefully framed. By focusing from the beginning on selection criteria and curriculum alignment, games can be established more easily and become a natural part of school libraries.

Games can provide an environment that naturally promotes learning through structured play. The ability of the game format to combine capacity for instructional support and personal fulfillment makes it an ideal resource for inclusion in a school library. The challenge then becomes one of gaining acceptance for a new type of resource that, like graphic novels, has often been portrayed as a less serious format lacking in instructional merit. Designer games, carefully selected using established criteria that place a high priority on authenticity and curriculum alignment, may be the best way for school libraries to demonstrate the potential for games.

Notes

1. Cathy De Rosa et al., *Perceptions of Libraries and Information Resources* (Dublin, OH: OCLC, 2005). Available at www.oclc.org/reports/2005perceptions.htm.
2. Scott Nicholson, "The Role of Gaming in Libraries: Taking the Pulse," 2007, www.boardgameswithscott.com/pulse2007.pdf.

PART II
Games for Twenty-First-Century Learners

This section will look at the ways in which games connect with both national and state learning standards. First, we'll look at how the gaming experience applies to library and information literacy skills. By drilling down within each of the concepts and looking at exactly how gaming connects to specific skills, we can establish a strong case for gaming as a curriculum-aligned part of library instruction. Along the way, we'll highlight specific games that build and develop the skills discussed in each of the major concept areas. Equally important are learning standards from the classrooms that libraries support.

The second part of this section will focus on the games and gaming concepts that align with English and language arts, science, social studies, math, and other curriculum areas. It is this alignment to both state and national standards that helps educators and administrators see the value that games have for the school environment. With accountability and performance levels set so high, resources must have a direct impact on a student's ability to be successful in his academic pursuits.

Library and
Information Skills

S chool librarians help students grow as learners in a variety of ways. They do so through providing a library space that welcomes learners and feeds their interests with a rich variety of resources, as well as through actions including collaboration, resource sharing, and coteaching. All of these things allow librarians to have a direct impact on student learning and achievement.

Ideally, librarians will have the budget to create a welcoming, well-stocked learning environment and the opportunities to collaborate with educators from across all curricular areas. When these come together, the school librarian can use her unique vantage point to strengthen each learning experience with an infusion of content and information literacy skills.

Included in the librarian's arsenal of available resources are games that, when played in the library, add to the invitational appeal of the space to students. And when they are used as an educational resource, games help students connect with the curriculum by making learning fun.

INFORMATIONAL IMPLICATIONS OF GAMING

As information grows more transitory, students need opportunities to engage in active information interactions by reading, decoding, analyzing, assessing, and taking action on information that is not static in nature. It is also important that students are exposed to informational experiences in media where they might not expect them. While traditional classroom activities have successfully addressed the needs of yesterday's information seekers, today's and tomorrow's seekers need more.

This is where games can help. They prepare students for this wider world of information by providing a platform for engagement through inquiry, all in an environment that is rich with content and fluid in nature. Games then become another information resource that, if selected appropriately, can meet the needs of many students, including those who can sometimes be missed by traditional classroom measures.

Games have the potential to serve as a learning platform because not only do they introduce informational and curricular skills in a complex and vibrant manner, but the inherent enjoyment of play also provides strong motivation for continued growth through student exploration and the refinement of those skills. This higher level of engagement can help students learn to persevere and, through repeated play, allow them to appreciate the validity of varying approaches to problems. Soon students come away with an understanding that differing approaches to inquiry can produce successful interactions with information. The fact that there is not always one way to approach and solve a problem becomes more apparent when students are confronted with situations of imperfect information and randomization, which are often utilized as game mechanics by designers. This, along with the oftentimes unpredictable nature of human choice, makes game play a continually unique and challenging experience.

SOCIAL IMPLICATIONS OF GAMING

The social nature of game play provides an opportunity for students to explore some real-world skills and realities, including ethical choices and their consequences when gathering and using information. Does a player cheat to gain a slight advantage at the risk of being caught and asked to leave the game? Does an experienced player dominate new players for the satisfaction of gaining another win? With games, students are presented the opportunity to learn from the negative consequences of unethical choices, in a less damaging environment, before they make the same bad choices in a classroom setting.

Information Processing 101

Another social implication is helping students strengthen their ability to process multiple sources of information with the immediacy necessary in today's digital culture. Today's technology society has created a "mash-up culture," with information presented in a variety of formats, from different sources, all aggregated into a single place. Common examples include a major news station with headline news commentary, stock returns, weather, and sports scores all running simultaneously, or a personal web page with video feeds, music, pictures, text, and animations. What can seem to some as information overload is becoming more common in today's information landscape.

In designer games, players must draw out information and build knowledge from graphical, social, audible, textual, and even hidden informational sources. This inquiry process may take the course of the entire game, a single turn, or mere moments. By selecting games with embedded curricular content and skills, educators can model how to locate and interact with this complex web of information while continuing to address the classroom curriculum.

With the wealth and variety of information at our students' fingertips, it is imperative not only to teach students how to navigate, but also how to effectively harvest the sea of information in which they find themselves adrift. Borrowing from an old adage, students need to be taught how to fish.

One of the ways in which this can be done is by providing access to selected gaming activities and supplemental online resources. By doing so, librarians are continuing to strengthen the development of the same information literacy skills that are usually taught in the context of research. Those skills can then be applied to activities in which the students have become emotionally invested. Through the use of the familiar and fun, games provide an experience that prompts the use of key skills central to each student's success in the future.

Today's community of learners has become more expansive than the classroom. This community is global, and membership requires students to participate socially, on a large scale, in a safe, informed, and effective manner. Whether interacting cooperatively or competitively, individuals playing games will develop and practice the skills necessary to successfully share and learn with others.

Personal Interaction Skills

With an increasing number of today's social interactions taking place online, students are at risk of losing the interactive experiences needed to build the face-to-face skills that are still relevant for their future success. This is why, when selecting gaming resources, schools should focus on gaming experiences that bring students together and foster social interaction.

Students can also serve as peer mentors, initiating other students who are unfamiliar with a game and providing advice on how to interpret and interact with information throughout the gaming experience. Here students can work as partners or coaches to provide real-time guidance and feedback as each inquiry situation presents itself. This is a particularly effective strategy to use with students who are English language learners. Because many designer games are language independent, this allows a new English speaker to learn a game and then serve as the teacher for other students.

User-driven resources like Board Game Geek (www.boardgamegeek .com) provide students an outlet to post and read information about the games they enjoy. Additionally, they have the ability to provide feedback and share their opinions through reviews, ratings, and tags. These resources can serve as a research base for the student's interests, allowing her the opportunity to begin the inquiry process before she sits down and starts playing a game. Students can research the best strategies or look for clarification on a poorly translated rule set. The exchange of information can continue after game play as students discuss and share their experiences with their peers.

One of the greatest strengths of online social networks and informational tools is the ability to connect individuals across the globe, effectively expanding the student's network of fellow learners. By providing opportunities for participation, school librarians and teachers are helping students develop the skills necessary to succeed in school and beyond.

LIBRARY AND INFORMATION SKILLS ALIGNMENT

The use of games and gaming in school libraries can be aligned to commonly accepted library and information skills. Selected areas of alignment are presented here to provide a general framework for understanding how games can be viewed within the context of school library instructional standards with an overarching focus on critical thinking skills. These alignments explain both the why and the how of building support for the use of games.

Inquiry

As educators, librarians help students develop the skills they need to successfully engage in genuine inquiry. They do so by selecting and providing resources that not only speak to the interests of the students but support the inquiry process as well. By including curriculum-aligned games in their resource collections, school libraries provide an avenue for applying the inquiry skills being developed in school that has meaning and context outside of what is seen by the students as the educational environment.

This happens because during play, students develop an investment in a game in direct relation to how much they enjoyed the game. Afterward, students will often purchase a game they enjoyed playing in school so that they can continue to play on their own time, sharing the experience with their friends. The game is no longer an educational activity confined to school but becomes an experience that they actively seek on their own time.

Games are also an excellent tool for empowering students to engage in self-directed inquiry and discovery at a young age. Because games provide a safe and familiar environment, students can gain the confidence to try different choices in their efforts to find a successful path. Students begin to independently participate in an environment of exploration with a structured value system and a set of rules that lay out expectations for behavior within the confines of the environment—along with consequences for poor decisions. Knowing what their goals are and what rules are governing the experience provides guidelines for students during the game. These guidelines are what help the students feel more comfortable taking risks and exploring different inquiry strategies.

Inquiry can begin at a very young age when supported by games. Fortunately, there are many highly engaging designer games being published for students from preschool age up. HABA is a German manufacturing company that produces high-quality games that engage even the youngest players. Playroom Entertainment and Blue Orange Games are publishing companies located in the United States that produce wonderful games for the same demographic. Combined, these three companies have challenged educators and parents to reevaluate their expectations of what a play experience can demand from a child. Time and again, parents and educators are surprised at how capable students are of rising to the occasion and engaging in more sophisticated gaming experiences. If we do not ask for more from our children, then how can we expect them to shine?

Inquiry is a required skill in many other games as well. Players need to maintain flexibility when developing and implementing strategies during game play. Because board and card games are an interactive activity, actions are not always predictable and the decisions needed are rarely the same with repeated plays. As a result, situations can and will change as a game progresses, requiring students to be flexible in the approaches and actions they take as they work toward achieving goals within the game.

These experiences help students build the confidence and skills needed to better cope with the unforeseen obstacles that are to be expected during inquiry and research activities. They can serve as transitions for students having difficulty moving from activities where resources and topics were hand selected for each student to ensure success, to activities where they need to accomplish these tasks on their own. Through repeated exposure, students learn to safely stumble, dust themselves off, and continue onward, perhaps on a new path or with a new goal in mind.

Game mechanics have also developed to support a more fluid game environment that favors inquiry. Today, designers will often use multiple mechanics within a single game, remaining sensitive to how each mechanic weighs in the game's overall playability. During game design, consideration is also given to how the game will scale with a different number of players and what victory conditions are necessary to trigger the game's end.

Having multiple victory conditions is a concept that is new to many who are unfamiliar with designer games. Games like Tribune provide some liberty in how overall victory is achieved. During a game, there are often many small problems, or steps, that require a convergent approach for success. In Tribune, players compete to control factions within ancient Rome. By controlling certain factions, players gain resources that combine to meet victory conditions. There are at least two ways to get every resource, however, so players have to stay flexible in their approach.

This is common in many designer games; victory points may be gained in many ways using combinations that are not explicitly defined. This freedom to explore different approaches toward victory rewards players who employ a divergent mind-set. Students have the freedom to explore the different combinations of actions available and, holding them up against the information encountered, select which choice works best for their current situation.

This combination of thought processes within a single learning experience helps strengthen the use of gaming as an inclusionary learning activity. By appealing to the strengths of students on both sides of the coin, it allows all players the opportunity to feel confident as they contribute to the learning community. Students are able to work comfortably from the perspective they are most familiar with while also developing and strengthening the other approach.

The intrinsic enjoyment that comes from playing games is also a powerful force in helping motivate students to demonstrate personal results through game growth and success. This is not necessarily measured by a student's rank at the end of the experience, but instead by the journey that brought them there. If you look closely, there is a valuable life lesson to be found in games: winning is not always necessary to be successful.

Designer games soften the schism created by the "lone victor" by shying away from player elimination. And despite a player's placement in the end, there are often smaller goals that, when completed, demonstrate a degree of success in acquiring the skills required to participate in the game. When those skills are curriculum related, then those successes mean even more; the game has helped the student demonstrate his mastery over a piece of the curriculum.

Along with the adaptability comes a need for resilience when searching for answers. Finding information has become less straightforward than in the past. With the growth of access to print, audio, and electric resources, the amount of information available can be overwhelming. With so many resource choices, students may not always know where to start their information endeavors nor how to adjust their approach when their initial attempts are not successful. Games offer positive experiences that can teach persistence and help students to learn that it is all right to fail. They walk away knowing that they can learn from their mistakes and still grow as learners. This is a hard lesson to impart in an environment where so much matters, but games succeed by providing an opportunity where students can fail and still continue on to succeed within a single learning experience.

The first time a student sits down at a table or picks up a controller, they do not expect—nor are they guaranteed—a successful gaming experience. Games often have a learning curve that builds toward proficiency. Initial plays are explorations in the system, becoming familiar with the

Featured Game

Ticket to Ride

© Days of Wonder, Inc.

Flexibility is the key to success in Days of Wonder's route-building train game Ticket to Ride. In the game, players work to complete routes on a map of the United States by connecting the two cities featured on each of the route cards in their hand. Although players may not be attempting to connect the same cities, they will be competing for the connecting cities in between as each works to complete his route.

As the game progresses, options become more limited as more of the connections between cities become claimed. As an example, one student may have been collecting the resources needed to connect Montreal and New York City to complete one of their route cards, when another player builds that connection before her turn. The original student now needs to reevaluate the resources available to her, both in her hand and on the board, to determine what alternative approaches she has available to help her reach her goal. She may need to shift which resources she is investing in so she can take a different route, or she may need to abandon this route and work on completing another one instead.

Apart from the geographical reinforcements, Ticket to Ride provides students with an opportunity to develop the flexibility and persistence needed when engaging in inquiry activities for both their academic and personal interests.

theme and mechanics of the game. However, students have the potential to excel within a game through a continual process of self-monitoring and adaptation of how they use information during their experience.

By actively monitoring their current strategies and choices, students can compare their progress to that of their peers. They are then able to modify future game play choices based on a comparative evaluation of their performance. This becomes particularly effective in games like Lost Cities, where each turn of the game consists of the same set of actions. Each player first selects a card from his hand to either discard or invest in one of five expeditions. Each card's value indicates the strength of the investment, with the goal being to raise the total investment in an expedition above twenty by the end of the game. Any expedition invested in whose total value could not be raised to twenty or higher counts negatively. After playing a card, players can then draw from one of the expedition's discard piles or the general draw pile. This process of play and draw is repeated until game's end, providing students the ability to effectively engage in self-monitoring behaviors within the short time frame of a single game.

By participating within learning communities, students have the opportunity to develop their inquiry skills through feedback and interaction with their teachers and peers. With guided game play, teachers can utilize selected gaming resources to introduce new skills or reinforce specific ones that need attention. One option is to use a game like Number Chase as a modeling situation, with the teacher using a think-aloud technique to walk the students through the skills needed to solve the problem. In Number Chase, there are cards with the numbers one to fifty printed on one side. These cards are laid in sequential order with the numbers facing up for all the players to see. One student secretly selects a number, while the other students actively work to deduce what that number might be. The other side of each card features a question to help the players narrow down the correct answer. Each student takes turns guessing the number. If they are incorrect, the number that was guessed is turned over, providing a question that the player with the secret number must truthfully answer (e.g., Is it an even number? Does it contain a three?). This experience provides the teacher with an opportunity to model how, starting with limited information, they are able to expand their knowledge and reach an answer through inquiry.

Students can also be encouraged to continue to engage in a pattern of inquiry through exploration of elements from games by reading books or other materials that provide additional background information. While a hard sell of books is not recommended as part of a gaming program, it is certainly a good idea to display or be ready to discuss books that align with the games being played.

Background Knowledge and Growth

Games can draw on a student's knowledge base through their themes to provide a strong anchor for learning. Most games utilize some form of a theme, using it to develop a setting or backstory that provides some context for the gaming experience. Students who already have knowledge of elements used within the game are able to bring that information to the table; this provides a starting point from which they can engage in the inquiry process, building and strengthening new knowledge along the way.

Featured Game

1960: The Making of the President

Used with permission from Z-Man Games, Inc.

1960: The Making of the President provides an excellent example of how, when students bring background knowledge into a game, it helps to facilitate inquiry and new learning. 1960 is a two-player game that re-creates the election of 1960 between presidential candidates John F. Kennedy and Richard Nixon. Players need to carefully balance their focus between the issues of the day, regional advertising, and campaigning in the states while being careful to avoid as much bad press as they can.

If students come into the experience with an understanding of the presidential electoral process in the United States and a basic familiarity with that time in our country's history, they will be able to start farther along the learning curve and draw more deeply from the gaming experience. What they've learned about the electoral process they will get to experience firsthand as they struggle to swing key states before the election. They will also get a deeper understanding of how the country's concerns regarding the economy, civil rights, and national security influenced the political landscape. Lastly, they will have an opportunity to compare that snapshot of American politics with what is happening today.

All of this is possible because students come into the experience with a foundation of knowledge upon which to build. They are able to take their understanding of U.S. politics and history and use it in a meaningful and engaging way, providing the opportunity for them to become personally invested in what they are learning in the classroom.

Games present a buffet of choices to players, with a variety of mechanics, themes, length, and playing styles available. As a result, students have an opportunity to try different experiences outside of their usual choices. Through dialogue with other students and an openness to experimentation, students are able to try out new experiences, take advantage of their peers' interests, and increase their exposure to different thematic content and skills.

Because many designer games are inclusionary and provide success opportunities beyond winning, initial ventures by students are rewarded with self-confidence and a desire to advance further with subsequent plays. Effective games inspire students to mentally revisit the events of their gaming experience, asking themselves key questions such as, "How did I do?" and "How can I be more effective the next time I play?" These questions provide guiding answers that help students grow as learners. Organizing the results for reflection, students are able to develop a direction for improvement in future games.

The community of play established by games, like many communities, creates a variety of roles that need to be filled. In each case, the choice is not made in isolation but is instead in response to the needs of the community. Students fall into opportune roles based on situational needs, taking on the guise of teacher, observer, participant, or mediator as needed. They may often wear several hats throughout a single gaming experience.

While students may naturally gravitate toward certain roles based on comfort and familiarity, educators can use games to expand their role repertoire. Each one can serve as a point for reflection and personal assessment, allowing students to gauge their ability to contribute to the group and respond to the contributions of others. By having exposure to a variety of ways in which individuals can effectively contribute to a learning experience, students are able to recognize their strengths and develop the approaches they are less comfortable with, resulting in more productive group interactions.

Evaluation of Information

Gaming provides an opportunity to practice the skill of information evaluation. Students actively participate in the gaming experience, taking in information to gather meaning and make inferences regarding motives, available resources, and potential actions. This information can manifest itself in a variety of formats within a game, with multiple formats being used concurrently.

With the increasing popularity of self-publishing on the Internet, the reliability of informational sources that students use is waning. Because of that, school librarians and educators are often on the lookout for engaging prompts for students to evaluate information. Games provide one such opportunity because they create a self-contained thematic experience, complete with guidelines for expectations and goals.

Successful game play requires each player to evaluate information observed during the gaming experience and for him to act upon that information based on the game's preset expectations. In other words, the game's rules define the context, value, and importance of the information, and the players need to use their skill set to evaluate and compare any information encountered to those set expectations.

There are many approaches to evaluating information, and different games can provide a learning experience for each of them. The evaluation of information based on its needs, importance, and appropriateness can be found in a game like Puerto Rico, where players need to work out which role or action would be most beneficial to choose based on the game's current situation. Battlestar Galactica, a cooperative game with a definite traitor, provides students the opportunity to weigh the accuracy, validity, and context of information by having them analyze social cues and behaviors to deduce the motivations and goals of their opponents.

Each of these examples brings about the need to question the importance and quality of information being encountered in a more casual activity. As educators, school librarians and teachers need to help their students not only understand these skills in the context of research, but also to help them put the skills into practice in their everyday lives. Games provide an activity that can allow students to see that the need to evaluate information is not limited to classroom activities. Instead, it transcends the curriculum, falling into the broader category of life skill.

A game's introductory information, such as directions, game mechanics, and thematic elements, can be conveyed textually or graphically. As play progresses, conversations and social cues can provide needed information for making decisions and building meaning within the constructs of the game. Regardless of the format, each player must deduce her opponent's strategy based on what actions have been taken and what potential moves may be available.

Rather than evaluating these sources in isolation, games require students to construct meaning through obvious and inferred informational sources and then synthesize a strategy for action based on the combined effect of all learned factors. This is a much higher level of interaction with informational sources than is typically demanded of students in an average classroom assignment.

Practicing and strengthening this skill early has the potential to help students prepare to effectively participate as twenty-first-century learners as they progress to the commencement and collegiate educational levels.

Games employ a variety of mechanics that require students to take a critical stance when making decisions based on information. Negotiation games such as Diplomacy provide opportunities for students to question the validity and accuracy of both the motives and information presented by other players. Shadows over Camelot utilizes a traitor mechanic that includes the possibility that one of the players might be playing with ulterior motives.

In both examples, students need to critically evaluate information from print and social sources to help them make decisions within the game. In these situations, students are able to explore the causal relationships behind why bias, self-interest, and misperception are used in the representation of information.

Use of Information

Unlike the cinema or television, a game does not just simply happen. In order to participate in the gaming experience, students need to interact with information encountered within the game. This need to interact in a critical yet enjoyable way is what defines a game.

Well-designed games make the experience engaging by defining varying degrees of complexity in interaction. They require players to approach information critically, utilizing it toward eventual mastery of the skills and content required for a successful gaming experience.

Additionally, while games may have thematic and mechanical connections to the curriculum, how that information comes together and interacts is often unique to each game experience. It requires students to analyze what information is being used in the game and to determine how much of their background knowledge will be of use. Students then need to combine their background knowledge and experiences with any new information provided in the game to synthesize a general inquiry approach and overall strategy. Throughout the course of the game, students will need to evaluate their progress to determine if they need to make any adjustments as they work toward their goals.

Because students are applying classroom content and skills to a unique environment, they are developing new understandings of the knowledge they already have. Additionally, new concepts and skills are being introduced in connection with game play, allowing students to build their knowledge base from their gaming endeavors.

In most games, players work from incomplete information. This means not everything is openly available, and often the information that is available may not be of obvious use. Players have to base their actions on conclusions drawn from what information is available at any given time. When those conclusions are drawn from information and skills aligned with the classroom curriculum, then additional opportunities arise for students to connect and apply knowledge gained during play back to their course work.

With the prevalence of designer games that do not make all the necessary information immediately open, information must often be drawn from any available sources. Clever games take advantage of mechanics and theme to provide a variety to the sources of information from which players draw.

Each source of information can operate differently, requiring students to use multiple inquiry strategies throughout the course of the game. After each step in the game, students will need to analyze their progress and determine if they have enough information to proceed or if they need to gather more information before developing their next step.

Featured Game

Chicago Express

Image supplied by Queen Games

Good games have multiple curricular points of entry for school librarians and teachers to use. By having connections to several different educational disciplines, a game can serve as a focal point for collaboration and student growth. Through the use of critical thinking and inquiry, students are able to make connections between the background knowledge they bring and new knowledge they are introduced to in the game. These originally disparate pieces come together over the course of the game to provide new insights and understanding for those involved, leaving students with a better understanding of the interconnectedness of knowledge.

Designed by Harry Wu, Chicago Express is an excellent example of this process in action. The game takes place in the years surrounding the birth of the major railways in the United States. Players invest in and develop several historical railroad companies, helping them grow and expand westward toward Chicago.

Over the course of play, students develop insight into the role economics played in the development and direction of U.S. history. The curricular entry point could be the westward expansion or basic economic investment. Either way, students marry both of these concepts as they develop their understanding of the game. And when they have finished, they will have strengthened the knowledge they brought and built new knowledge and understanding through active inquiry and critical thinking during the play process.

The game experience itself also demands flexibility in where information is gathered and how it is utilized. Potential sources of information include other players, the game itself, past play experiences, and suggested strategies for play. How much each source factors into the player's decisions varies with each game. Additionally, factor in that many games offer a variety of paths to victory and you now have a very fluid learning environment.

All games require players to take action, but how information is acted upon depends on experience, exposure, and opportunity. What applicable background knowledge and previous experiences do the players bring to the table? How much information do they have openly available to them? What needs to be inferred or speculated? And lastly, what opportunities do students have to access and evaluate the information?

Many of these answers are determined by the mechanical elements the designer uses in the game. How they choose to make information available influences the actions of students as they are playing. Games based around imperfect information do not have a full reveal of everything within the game. This leaves the students with a more critical approach to their inquiry and explorations because information has a much greater potential for misinterpretation and speculation. This is in stark contrast to a game that provides perfect information. Here students will adopt a more analytical mind-set when taking action.

School librarians and teachers can use gaming resources to create different informational situations for students. Perfect information games, such as Hive, can be used to allow students to focus on assessing the information available, determining possible outcomes, and developing a sequence of actions. Other situations can be created using imperfect information games, helping students strengthen their evaluative and inferential skills. In either situation, by taking advantage of game design elements educators are able to help their students grow as informational decision makers.

The Time Factor

An additional design factor that influences student decision making is time. How much of an opportunity do students have to examine, evaluate, and act upon information? Game play may provide students with opportunities for careful consideration, or their decisions may need to occur at an instinctual level, with little time for foresight and planning. While perfect information may provide everything a student needs to reach her goals, if timed turns force each decision to be rushed, then actions can more easily fall prey to poor decisions. Compare the difference in approach between a game of chess that is timed and one that is not. Regardless of how expeditious students need to be, there is still a necessity for informational assessment and action during play.

Long-Term Thinking

There is a growth cycle of learning that takes place during game play. As play progresses, students need to continually shift their focus between their immediate needs and their long-term goals. Many of the long-term goals in games can be complex and require constant evaluation of the player's progress toward meeting them. This type of evaluation provides the opportunity for students to develop new directions of investigation in an effort that will lead to a final solution.

Breaking this process down, each time a student prepares to take an action during a game, she assesses her progress toward any goals. If she has not yet met her goals, she needs to analyze the information she has available, tempering it with her experience and checking to determine if she has built any new understandings that may help her move forward. This process provides perspective for students when developing strategies for future investigations. Students may decide to synthesize a new strategy, modify their current one, or stay the course. Once decided, students take action and start the cycle again, repeating until the game's conclusion.

While each piece of this process can be addressed individually, it is as a whole that they reflect the value that gaming has as an educational resource. Just as individual library skills can be taught in isolation, it is the sum of their parts put into practice that demonstrates their true merit.

COLLABORATIVE LEARNING

Collaboration and socialization can have a strong influence on both the academic success and motivation of students. Knowing this, the challenge for school librarians and educators becomes finding effective prompts for initiating these types of learning experiences. Games naturally elicit social interaction and so can provide a comfortable platform for students to engage in collaboration. With individuals discussing and working in teams, students have the opportunity to deepen their understanding not only of the content and skills involved with the activity but of each other as well.

By participating in collaborative activities around games, students are more likely to take risks and explore alternative viewpoints because they are in a familiar and fun environment. This comfort level helps educators scaffold students to develop successful participatory experiences and an inclusionary approach when striving for success. The wide variety of designer games that use a cooperative mechanic provides another way for libraries to focus on the power of collaboration. Lord of the Rings demands a high level of collaboration, with players having to share cards to meet conditions as the game progresses.

Students can also participate collaboratively in the game experience by offering advice and leadership during cooperative play or giving feedback and suggestions after decisions are made while engaged in competitive activities. Student contributions can also take place away from the table as they discuss strategies related to the game. A more obvious focus on the curriculum can be achieved through the use of guided prompts, allowing students to contribute to discussions regarding how curricular content is used within the game. This can be done by the school librarian or teacher, either as an anticipatory set entering into game play or as a reflective piece afterward.

On a larger scale, it is also important to remember that being a part of a learning community is no longer confined within the walls of the school. Students can also be encouraged to participate and engage in discussions online, either in educator-created online environments or an open community web space. Games provide the opportunity for students to work with and observe other students interacting with information and solving problems. Students are not dealing with an isolated snapshot of strategies but instead are able to see them solidify within a learning environment. What information was important, when, and why? What problem-solving strategies worked? What events or actions precipitated and resulted from successful choices?

During a game, students become members of a constructed community of play whose rules of conduct and interaction differ from more traditional social situations. One of those differences is the desire to engage in good-natured banter. Often, when students are successful in finding answers or solving problems, they do not refrain from sharing that information. While this may sometimes take the form of lighthearted bragging or boasting, it is still a valuable learning experience for the rest of the players involved.

In an educational setting, this banter can be redirected in a more productive manner by encouraging students to reflect on and share their successes throughout the game so that others can learn from their approach to problems. In most cases, each of the participating players has the same goals with similar challenges and choices to be made. As those challenges arise and choices are made, unless they are identical, each player's path toward a successful resolution will diverge from the others.

This overlap and division create points of reference for the students to reflect on, comparing inquiry approaches and choices. They also establish a shared experience framework around which students can learn and grow through discussion and dialogue. This is another way in which the norms for interaction can deviate within a community of play. Members are more willing to share strategies and advice with others in an effort to improve the quality of the experience. By helping each other, players are working to provide a more challenging and rewarding experience for themselves.

Whether in the classroom or online, games facilitate the sharing of concepts and strategies through collaboration among players and an active reflection on personal performance. These moments of interaction and collaboration are not confined to sporadic moments of socialization but instead transpire throughout the course of the game. Starting when more experienced students help newer players become familiar with the rules, a community of play is created. This community continues with collaboration and advice given during play and concludes as students discuss post-game reflections and musings. Games lower the barrier for membership in a network of learners. This is not to say that the quality of interactions is less, but instead the effort required to gain entry is minimized. Simply by participating in a gaming experience, students earn their citizenship and begin to benefit from the support and shared exchange of ideas.

The classroom is full of formal opportunities for presentation. Games, and play itself, provide a powerful scaffolding platform for preparing students to be successful in presentational situations. These activities allow the temporary removal of student-constructed social barriers, providing a level of comfort that helps students to develop leadership skills and build the confidence to present ideas to others.

By taking their first steps within the relative safety of a game, students learn to trust their instincts and voice their opinions. They learn to speak out with confidence, arguing persuasively based on inquiry and the critical analysis of information within the game. Cooperative games provide students practice at lending their voice to group decisions. If the game utilizes the traitor mechanic or role-playing, students may need to argue their case to the rest of the players, attempting to persuade, curry favor, and beguile the opposition. (Educators can use the strong thematic elements or even reflections on the gaming experience itself to provide a host of discussion points for formal presentational ideas with a class.)

Games can help students understand that not only can they participate, but they should. Sports has shown the value of teamwork, demonstrating how each member contributes to the success of the team. When a player does not try to his full potential, students soon learn that it is to the detriment of his peers playing alongside him.

Most schoolwork stands in stark contrast to this, with individual achievement being a primary focus. Through the use of curriculum-aligned games, school librarians and teachers can channel the social lessons and work ethics learned from structured sports activities into planned educational situations targeting select educational concepts and skills.

Games also bring along some inherent benefits that make them more attractive than scholastic competitions. Games are dynamic, allowing

Featured Game

Shadows over Camelot

© Days of Wonder, Inc.

Shadows over Camelot is an adventure on a grand scale. Players take on the role of one of Camelot's Knights of the Round Table, working together as they struggle to defend Camelot from the enemies that hope to see it fall. As with most cooperative games, the enemy the students face is the game itself.

One of the strengths of this game is its ability to bring together groups of students who would not normally interact on their own. Shy students start to come out of their shells to offer their assistance and advice to the group, while headstrong players soon learn that they sometimes need to rely on others to succeed.

Aside from reinforcing the Arthurian mythos, the game also serves as a resource for school librarians and teachers to develop group work skills with their students. Shadows over Camelot creates a meaningful experience within the context of the gaming environment. Because this game requires cooperation, communication, and self-sacrifice, the experience has the potential to elicit more genuine developmental opportunities than traditional group activities. Students begin participating through play, adopting the norms and guidelines created by the gaming experience. When those norms require an approach that favors teamwork, students are willing to work within those boundaries. It is that motivation, coupled with necessity, that makes cooperative games so effective in helping students grow.

students the opportunity to build and then apply information to unique situations, while competitions usually favor the memorization and recall of information already known. Additionally, the majority of designer games are inclusive, allowing everyone to participate throughout the experience, while competitions usually work by process of elimination.

With the inclusion of educational activities structured around select games, school librarians and teachers are able to set the stage for participation by immersing students in learning situations that provide the needed experiences to help social responsibility develop.

Cooperative Games

Certain games help students develop collaborative skills by demanding effective teamwork from the players if they are going to be successful. Cooperative games are a specific subset of gaming that uses teamwork as the primary driving factor for game play. While more traditional cooperative games such as Lord of the Rings or Shadows over Camelot come with a longer play time, their return on investment is high, providing a rich experience and unique opportunities for social interaction.

Cooperative games are unique. They require students to actively work together, freely exchanging ideas, information, and resources in order for the group to be successful against the mechanics of the game. By participating in these cooperative learning experiences, students are able to take part in collaborative groups and observe other players model successful choices. These experiences have a positive effect on future problem-solving efforts by the students, helping them grow as learners by providing them with a reference point when making choices of their own.

Recently, there has been an increase in the number or cooperative games available. Perhaps adding to this game genre's popularity is a refinement in play mechanics that has brought play down to a more accessible time frame of about one hour; Pandemic and Ghost Stories are prime examples of this trend.

Most cooperative games pit the students against the game, allowing little room for mistakes. Without communication and coordination, players will quickly begin to lose their footing and students will learn that unless they truly work together, they will never be able to achieve success.

Real-World Connections

A game's theme is what often draws in and connects with a student. Clever mechanics can do this too, but not as often as theme. Conceptually, you can compare a game's theme to genre in literature. People will more often profess a preference for a particular genre than, say, a writing style.

Game themes run the gamut from the abstract (chess is a very abstract re-creation of a battlefield) to the detailed. On the detailed end of the spectrum, game designers can weave rich tapestries that successfully immerse the player in a particular time and place or simulate a certain set of circumstances. While some themes aim to educate or entertain, others transcend the table, providing students with insight into issues that can have both relevance and personal meaning to their lives. Political, economic, and environmental topics are not uncommon thematic elements used in designer games, each of which has the potential to generate personal affect.

Power Grid

© Rio Grande Games

Power Grid is an example of a game that grows beyond the simplicity of its theme to engage students in topical matters of importance. In the game, players are working to expand the network of cities they supply power to by purchasing different power plants and the resources needed to run them. The more cities students are able to power, the more money they can make. The winner is the player who can power the most cities after the end-game condition has been met. While this may not initially stand out as having strong educational ties, the brilliance of the game as an educational tool lies in the details built into the mechanics and theme.

First, students need to bid on power plants, which can use a variety of different resource types. Which plants are available can depend on the map being used by the players. The base game comes with a map of the United States and Germany, but there are additional maps available with custom rule modifications that reflect the energy and market situations of that region. To match the controlled Chinese market, that map uses a preset upgrade path for power plants as a thematic element to match reality.

After bidding on a plant, students purchase the resources needed to power their plants from the open market. Fossil fuels are abundant and inexpensive at the beginning of the game, making them a wise choice to start. As the game progresses, though, they do not get replenished as frequently. This can cause the cost to purchase fossil fuels to jump drastically as the supply cannot meet the demand. Students who have relied too heavily on fossil fuels can find themselves unable to purchase the resources needed to power the cities on their grid, leaving them to fall behind in the game.

By using these thematic and mechanical nuances, Power Grid allows students to experiment with economic and environmental concepts in an environment where situations can easily mirror those found in news headlines. They become involved in what they are learning, not only exploring common economic situations but actively contributing to their development. Power Grid helps to show that given proper guidance, game experiences can serve as a bridge between what students learn in the classroom and what they see happening in the world.

These games can then be used as springboards for conversations surrounding important topics of the day. If the game is well designed, the students will not simply be learning about these topics but will experience and interact with them. They can have the opportunity to see how ideas like equality, ideology, supply and demand, resource scarcity, energy consumption, and religion can have an effect on situations and circumstances. And in the end, these experiences help students grow as learners by adding to their understanding of how these ideas connect in the real world.

Students also gain a broader real-world perspective when they find themselves outside of their culture, facing problems that may require them to consider alternative viewpoints and perspectives. Providing authentic opportunities for this type of inquiry can prove difficult, but games provide a pathway toward that goal similar to the way that literature does.

Both games and literature use the elements of setting and theme to immerse the participant in an experience. While books have writers, games are created by designers—and many of these designers come from countries and cultures with which students are unfamiliar. Like multicultural literature, through the use of theme, setting, and the designer's heritage, games present students with situations and problems that may require a more globally sensitive perspective to achieve a successful experience.

A wonderful example is Martin Wallace's Brass, which introduces students to historical Lancashire, England, during the Industrial Revolution. The combination of theme, period styled artwork, the use of the English monetary system, and Mr. Wallace's English heritage create an immersive environment in which students feel a part of the eighteenth-century industrial boom.

Well-designed games can be breathtaking. The right marriage of theme and mechanics provides an engaging and ultimately rewarding experience. Through the use of well-developed themes, games can connect ideas to the interests of students and build upon knowledge and experiences developed in the classroom.

A common goal of school librarians and teachers is to elicit genuine dialogue from students in regard to classroom content. When educators use preselected, curriculum-aligned games as a facilitating medium, students' interests are sparked while their curricular needs are being met. Once an interest has been created, students are more apt to contribute to the learning community that is created within the game, as well as within the classroom and beyond. While students may believe they are simply discussing their experiences with the game, because of the curricular connections, they are also reinforcing content and skills they are learning in the classroom.

With a wealth of thematic topics, designer games are capable of meeting the interests and needs of students while reinforcing the content and skills sought by educators: games can connect to literature—Pillars of the Earth and Lord of the Rings are based on the books of the same name. Popular culture and opinion is commonly seen in party games such as Wits and Wagers and Time's Up! Title Recall!. Ancient civilizations are reflected in Through the Ages; American history drives Manifest Destiny; farming and agriculture themes Agricola; science fiction stars in Race for the Galaxy; auto racing is the stage for Bolide . . . the list stretches on and on.

Games provide opportunities beyond the immediacy of this week's lesson. Student growth through game play and exploration extends to life skills, and discovered knowledge can spark an interest in other areas of study, making history, geography, math, and science topics of interest when they were not before. Social skills are developed as students learn to more effectively collaborate, make independent choices, work in teams, take turns, share, and stay open to different ideas and perspectives. And lastly, students build the skills needed for future inquiry, making persistence, independence, and adaptability a part of their inquiry repertoire.

Alignment with State and National Curriculum Standards

Alignment is crucial for building understanding and acceptance for the use of games in an educational setting. With No Child Left Behind and the shift in education toward testing, time has become a valuable commodity in the classroom. Teachers are now more accountable than they have ever been, and classroom activities must focus on building the necessary skills and content knowledge that enable students to achieve success.

It then becomes vital that students have a vested interest in their learning, that they internalize, organize, and interpret what the educational system demands of them. The more involved they are with the content they are immersed in, the more likely they are to be successful. Designer games leverage the social interaction and inherent fun of play to provide a powerful motivator for learning and growth. By selecting games that introduce and reinforce content and skills from the curriculum, we can harvest play's motivational power to help our students grow and be successful.

There is no proper way to connect students with the curriculum except the way that works. Literature is often used in the content areas to enhance and bring meaning to the subject studied. Again, games can easily fill that niche as well. Many designer games meet the learning needs of educators and, in a broader sense, so does the gaming experience itself. While they may not quite live up to the strength of personal narratives, games do help students connect with areas by allowing them to create their own narratives through play. Ancient civilizations, political processes, energy choices, and economic principles are just some of the learning opportunities awaiting students with games. Games also provide a context and meaning for many of the math, science, and English and language arts (ELA) skills that students work with each day.

This chapter will look at the ways in which games and the gaming experience connect with national and state learning standards. Four key curricular areas (ELA, social studies, mathematics, and science) will be addressed, and along the way specific games will be highlighted that build and develop the skills discussed in each curricular area. While only these four content areas will be addressed, this does not imply that games do not apply to other areas as well. The selected areas are simply representative of the heart of a student's classroom experiences and provide prime examples of how designer games meet the needs of classroom learners.

ENGLISH AND LANGUAGE ARTS

Reading and a student's literacy ability have consistently shown a strong correlation to school performance. There can be no doubt of the importance they play in a student's educational future. Now those skills and abilities are being reexamined as new measures are being sought to supplement more traditional approaches. Activities being used in schools to introduce and strengthen literacy are expanding to include more nontraditional experiences; students are being asked to subject electronic and nonprint texts to the same skill sets applied to poetry and fiction. So it becomes important that students are exposed to new literacy experiences and learning to apply classroom skills across a variety of media.

Just as with any other resource, designer games provide multiple entry points to the ELA curriculum. The challenge for educators is to find the ways in which these potential new resources support student learning. How do they address both traditional and more contemporary needs? One of the strengths of designer games is their ability to support both.

Traditional student benchmarks and expectations for performance come from the standards set at the state and national levels. These standards provide a set of guidelines for literacy and language skills that will serve as the bedrock for much of a student's academic success. Inherent in the standards are the abilities and tools needed to successfully engage with communication, whether oral, visual, or in print. Standards at the national level serve as a best practices model, while each state provides their own set of standards that are used in the classroom.

Designer games, holding many parallels to literature, easily meet many of the traditional ELA curricular needs, while providing a unique approach to these learning experiences. Within these games, there are opportunities to build and deconstruct stories; to explore story elements of genre, characters, plot, and settings, as well as the people who created them; to establish the basic literacy skills needed for reading and writing; to develop and strengthen students' vocabulary base; and to explore the emotional nuances of language, including persuasion and critical evaluation.

Storytelling

One does not have to look too far to find elements of storytelling within designer games. Characters and backgrounds, plots and subplots, problems and resolutions—all of these elements can be found within the designer game experience. Even at a simple and more familiar level, Clue presents a tale of mystery and murder, but there are no real backgrounds provided for the characters and there is little opportunity for them to develop through play.

Modern designer games feature storytelling through story-building games and games with story involvement. Story-building games, such as Nanofictionary and Once upon a Time, can empower students to develop and showcase their story-crafting skills. Through the mechanical combination of story elements, these games provide the tools and prompts for students to construct their own tales. For example, in Once upon a Time, players tell fairy tales using the cards they have in their hands. One player is the storyteller, weaving a tale by playing cards down to match prominent elements in the story being told, while the other players actively listen. If the storyteller mentions an element that another player has a card for, that player can play her card and take over the story. Additionally, if the storyteller plays a card for an element that is just mentioned in passing, the other players can object and pick up the story line. The stories are a small part of the experience and do not mark it as deeply as in other games. Instead, the focus is on the use of elements to build stories that entertain more than engage.

Other games provide varying levels of story involvement, usually through a combination of mechanics and theme. These games allow students the opportunity to participate in the experience, guiding the game's narrative through social interactions and game choices. While the story may develop from the actions taken by the player, like a go-kart ride, the students only have control within a closed and guided environment.

Cooperative games such as Battlestar Galactica, Shadows over Camelot, Ghost Stories, Lord of the Rings, and Pandemic establish a strong plot that plays out over the course of the game. While the boundaries of the story are well defined, it is the player interactions inherent in cooperative games that generate the intrigue. The progression of the plot and tension built make each event memorable as students struggle together, communicating and sharing in a community of play.

Competitive games can also tell a story through well-developed game design. 1960: The Making of the President recounts the famed election of that year; Android presents a dystopian mystery akin to *Blade Runner;* Prophecy, World of Warcraft, and other role-playing games allow students to invest in and develop characters through interactions with the game environment; and ancient civilization games like Antike, Amun-Re, and Tribune present students an opportunity to play a part in the world's history. Again, students are working from point to point within a preestablished narrative, but these games focus on the interplay of actions for the game's progression. One example is Pillars of the Earth, a game based on the Ken Follett novel in which students work to build the Kingsbridge

Cathedral. A good worker placement game, the backstory and time frame of Pillars of the Earth are well established. It is the blending of choices, the proactive and reactive selecting of actions, that brings to life and carries the narrative to the end. But with all of the aforementioned games, options are limited to the actions and elements contained within the game experience. This differs from a small subset of storytelling games: social games.

Social games, such as Ultimate Werewolf, are less defined and therefore less confining than other game experiences. By only providing some very basic roles and rules, they allow students to actively construct and be a part of the gaming experience. Progression of the game's narrative is much more dependent on the students participating. (This can be a disadvantage with players who are not willing to let go and immerse themselves in the game.)

Whether overt or subtle, there exists in games a valuable resource for engaging students with the beauty of stories. Besides sharing many elements with literature, games give students the opportunity to be a part of a story. Their explorations and actions build ownership of their learning environment as they reflect, create, and grow as members of a literacy community.

Building and Using Literacy Skills

Any opportunity for students to put in practice word and language skills is a valuable opportunity for their growth as learners. There are many authentic games that touch on the literacy skills developed at the elementary and middle school levels. Some games focus on mechanics—the building and strengthening of specific literacy skills—while other games facilitate the use of these skills through conversation and player interactions.

Looking at the mechanics of literacy, games like My Word and Quiddler strengthen word-building and vocabulary skills as students use word elements to build phonics and phoneme strength. LetterFlip targets similar skills as students work through word families and spelling patterns to deduce mystery words in a fun variation of hangman. Another game, M is for Mouse, helps students strengthen beginning letter recognition skills as they try to match letters and pictures from cards in their hands with letters and pictures from a card on the table. All of these games provide a fun and engaging vehicle for basic literacy skills that can help struggling students build their way toward mastery or provide a refreshing review for a whole class.

While the building of skills is a necessary step toward literacy, the practical application of those skills is equally important for student growth.

Because of play's ability to elicit genuine interest from students, their contributions and efforts can often be some of their best. The combination of these elements allows students the comfort and confidence to engage with their peers in a variety of interactive situations. Drawing games like Portrayal and Back Seat Drawing require the use of both descriptive language on the part of the student talking about a picture and active listening for those students drawing.

Cooperative games allow for a motivated use of persuasive language as students work together, contributing ideas and making their case for the best course of action throughout the game. At an elementary level, cooperative games like Max and Orchard focus on teaching younger students to work together and respect different ideas and approaches to solving problems. As students progress in grade, the social experiences of cooperative games mature as well. Battlestar Galactica and Shadows over Camelot extend the cooperative experience further with the inclusion of a traitor. Now students must balance the need for teamwork with a level of mistrust, critically evaluating the actions and information presented by both the game and other players.

With each game experience, students are building and refining literacy skills so critical to their academic success that to dismiss gaming because of prejudice is inexcusable. The goal is to inspire students to develop their mastery over the English language regardless of format. School libraries have seen how graphic novels have reached a population of students that have otherwise been reluctant readers. By extending that openness to other alternatives, teachers and librarians will find the value that games bring as well.

ELA for English Language Learners

Support for English-language-learner programs and the needs of their students can be found throughout the designer game experience. Games can help build basic English literacy skills, like those covered above, or they can offer more sophisticated experiences that promote the use of language in a communicative and interactive manner. Showing their European heritage, many designer board games are built to be language independent; after the rules are learned, the boards and playing pieces in many games use pictograms instead of words to allow multilingual editions. Language-independent games like Ticket to Ride and Amun-Re offer opportunities for English language learners in middle school to participate in high-quality and engaging learning experiences without being restricted by a language barrier. Many of the higher-order thinking activities in schools are based on reading and writing, so this gives these students a way to interact with the curriculum in an effective and lasting manner.

SOCIAL STUDIES

So much falls under the umbrella of the social studies curriculum. Students need to see the importance of past events and how they influence us today. They need to recognize the shape and history of the land and understand how geography can affect culture and development. They also need to develop a knowledge of government and finance, seeking the ethics and morality behind the rules. In all of these areas, the strength of games is their ability to engage students with the curriculum by letting them interact and play a part. Games have the ability to tap into the shared social experience, draw from history, and re-create a window into our past, bringing the world and its story to the student's table.

Some games have a very strong and direct connection to curriculum, while others may be more incidental, merely capturing the flavor of a time or place. Additionally, games can be very focused or may address a variety of curricula. For example, the 10 Days series specializes in the geography of a particular region, while 1960: The Making of the President brings together history, geography, and civics and combines them into one rich experience. Regardless of the details, through the use of well-developed themes, games are able to bring to life places and moments that helped shape who we are and where we are heading.

Ancient Civilizations

There are many aspects that can be addressed when studying ancient civilizations: culture, religion, politics, and war were all factors that helped shape and guide their growth and decline. While designer games may not always present a fully accurate account, they do go far in capturing elements that can be used to enrich and reinforce the classroom curriculum. From Egypt through Rome and Greece to China, games can take students over land and through time, making the past matter.

Amun-Re allows students to exert influence over ancient Egypt, building and developing land along the banks of the Nile River. Each plot of land varies depending on its relationship to the Nile, with more fertile areas closer to the water. Students play through two rounds, the Old Kingdom and the New Kingdom, and between rounds all developments are erased from the board with the exception of the pyramids, which carry over through time. Amun-Re helps remind students of the importance of agriculture and religion to the Egyptians, as well as allows them to contribute to the legacy of Egyptian architecture.

Ancient Rome was a robust and complex civilization, making it difficult to encapsulate in a single gaming experience. There are many games that can help flesh out different aspects of Roman culture and life for students. Tribune is a game about the ascension to political power within the social and cultural potpourri that had developed within the empire as a result of its growth and expansion. As players set their eyes on a rise in power, they can only do so with the favor and backing of different factions within Rome's social strata. In addition to this, the game also brings along a wealth of period vocabulary, making it a valuable asset for a unit of study on Roman life.

While Tribune focuses on Roman politics and social structure, Colosseum tackles its taste in entertainment as students play Roman impresarios attempting to put on the most impressive events for spectators, consuls, and even the emperor. Players have five turns to put on the most extraordinary spectacle possible. Prior to each event, students have the opportunity to expand their arena and purchase props, exotic animals, and combatants in an effort to put on larger and more impressive shows. Again, this is a game of vocabulary reinforcement and concept expansion. Students are reminded that the shows put on were more than gladiatorial matches; they were showcases of humor, history, epic tales, and culture.

Finally, Antike is a game of balance as players try to manage an empire during the eras of Rome and Greece. In the game, play draws attention to the geography of the people involved, prompting discussion on the influence that location had on the interactions of these great cultures. Students are also given an opportunity to engage in a more realistic example of empire expansion, as growth during the game is a balance of settling, conquest, urban development, and investment in technology.

The History of the World, Part II

As students read about the past, they begin to make connections among events, people, and places. To help make these things more meaningful and real, a variety of resources are available for use in the classroom. Movies and books are often used to help personalize the past, putting names, faces, and stories with the moments that define an era. Designer games can easily be added as an additional resource for connecting students with the curriculum. With their combination of history and narrative, they provide a well-balanced blend between entertainment and education.

Stone Age presents prehistoric man's daily struggles as he sheds his nomadic lifestyle and begins to settle down. Players are trying to help their tribe grow and survive by collecting resources, building settlements and farms, developing tools, and feeding their people. The game's mechanic for collecting resources is useful for helping students understand the uncertainties faced in such a primitive environment. Each turn, players place some of the people from their tribe onto resource spaces in hopes of gathering those resources. For each person placed, the student gets to roll a six-sided die. Each resource has a different value that is required for its collection. Students roll the dice for each resource, collecting as many resources as possible based on how many times the resources value goes into the total of the die roll. Players can use any tools they have developed to increase their ability to collect resources by augmenting their rolls.

Brass captures many aspects of the Industrial Revolution: the progression in efficiency, the dependency on resources, and the reliance on transportation for getting raw materials to the factories and finished products out for sale. Students play through two eras, the canal and rail eras. Each turn they spend their income building up their industry, improving production efficiency, expanding the network of canals and rails, and selling manufactured cotton to distant markets and private ports. Students must learn to work within this system, seeking to make their fortune in a new age of industry.

Looking at U.S. history, the early rail explosion is portrayed in the game Chicago Express, a game of development and growth that features pioneer railroad companies and their expansion westward. Jumping ahead to the twentieth century, both Twilight Struggle and 1960: The Making of the President use primary source images and historic events to create strong historical game experiences. In 1960, students have a chance to change the outcome of the historic campaigns of John F. Kennedy and Richard Nixon. Twilight Struggle, another game by the same designer, examines the great global dance that was the Cold War. Players in Twilight Struggle play the United States or Russia, the two great superpowers seeking to spread their ideology and politics throughout the world.

Through the Ages is a more ambitious game that gives students the opportunity to develop their own civilization from antiquity to modern times. Here students are able to progress through humanity's development in key areas such as technology, religion, culture, government, and leaders. As the game proceeds, new technologies and ideas are made available, new leaders and historical figures emerge to provide guidance, and new wonders can be built to provide benefit and inspire awe. Through play students can try different approaches with their civilizations and see how they interact with the approaches of other players. Another benefit is that students are able to step back and see the world's progression in a much shorter time frame than they would during the course of a class. It is a great way to bring together all of the individual pieces of history and show how they fit together.

Other games of note include España 1936, a light military game that covers the Spanish civil war, and Here I Stand, an epic game covering the Wars of the Reformation, featuring such notable historical figures as Martin Luther, John Calvin, Magellan, Cortés, Copernicus, and more.

Economics

There are a number of wonderful games that complement the study of economics, taking things much further than traditional games of finance such as Monopoly, Career, and Life. Instead, these designer games excel in providing a playable experience surrounding a single aspect or principle. This focus allows educators to select specific games as they progress through the curriculum. Power Grid is a game of energy production that features a strong example of a free market system. After bidding for power plants, students purchase the necessary resources to power their plants from the open market. Students soon learn the effects of supply and demand as well as the pitfalls of being overly dependent on a single resource as costs rise and the supply is limited.

Chicago Express serves as a light introduction to stocks, as students play the role of investors in railroad companies trying to make the most money on their investments. In the game, students don't own any of the railroad companies but instead become holders of shares, receiving dividends based on the value of the company every few turns. The benefits of holding a share in a company is that it gives the player rights to develop that company. Development money comes not from a player's personal assets but from the money that was invested in the company from the purchase of its shares. The money is then used to further develop the company, increasing its value and therefore the dividends paid out based on that value.

Puerto Rico is a game of economic development in which players are plantation owners on the title island trying to develop their business more effectively than their opponents. Players plant crops, process them into goods, and then can sell them on the market for money or ship them back to Europe for victory points. Students get an opportunity to interact with a simple model for the production, consumption, and distribution of goods and services.

Geography

Geography goes beyond names and places to examining how the earth has developed, its physical characteristics, and the effects these have had on human growth and progress.

When looking at games that focus on physical geography, there are two categories of games: those with detail and those with generality. The 10 Days series falls into the first category. It's a game of making connections; students take turns drawing and playing cards as they attempt to make a sequential arrangement of locations to complete a ten-day journey. There are four games in the series, each focusing on a different geographic locale with detailed maps serving as the game board. Each turn, students must continually reference the map as they try to find the location of the country or state tile they drew and where it lies in relation to the cards they already have. In addition, each card features an outline of the country, its approximate population, and square mileage. All of these features make for a curricularly rich experience for the students.

Many other games provide students a more casual reinforcement of geography. They usually feature less detailed maps that are not the primary focus of the game. Pandemic has students traveling the globe as they struggle to contain disease outbreaks while searching for a cure. Ticket to Ride and Ticket to Ride: Europe are train games where students work to connect cities to complete train routes. While all of the games feature maps, they are not a detailed representation of the area. Still, throughout each of the games students work within these geographical areas, internalizing and interacting with them in the context of play.

Geography can also be approached from a historical perspective, examining the land's influence on mankind's development or comparing how it has changed over time. Amun-Re, Brass, and 1960: The Making of the President look at geography from a historical perspective. Amun-Re demonstrates the importance that the Nile River played in Egypt's growth as well as how the characteristics of the land, and its use, changed the farther away you moved. Brass focuses on the era of the Industrial Revolution in Lancashire, England, where players are dependent on canals, and later railways, for helping move the raw materials to their factories as well as the finished products to available ports. They must work within the physical constraints of the area, using the natural waterways and coastal areas for transport and shipping. Lastly, adding to the realism and accuracy of the election in 1960 is a game board featuring an electoral map of the United States. The board itself features each of the fifty states and their electoral vote status at the time of the election. By comparing the electoral votes featured on the game board to today's, students are able to see how population has shifted over the last fifty years.

These are just a few examples to show the potential that designer board games have to connect students with a range of global, historical, and geographic concepts. Games lift these concepts from the page and make them interactive and more tangible for the students. When they are used in conjunction with additional resources such as literature, media, and electronic databases, they help to form a well-rounded unit that meets the needs of many different styles of learners.

MATHEMATICS

To truly grasp mathematics requires a delicate dance of concept and practice. Students not only need to learn mathematical concepts and principles, they also need to have continual opportunities for their use. Like any skill left stagnant, much of math can quickly fade from a student's repertoire. To keep math relevant and fresh, students need exposure to a variety of activities that are memorable and engaging. Play's inherent fun allows students to benefit from the practice without feeling the drain of rote lessons. This gives more students the opportunity to come to appreciate the beauty that is mathematics in action.

Multiplication, Division, Addition, and Subtraction

These are the most basic and prevalent math skills found in games. Traditionally, these skills are used when tallying scores or calculating finances in familiar games like gin rummy or Monopoly. But there are a variety of great games available that incorporate these fundamental skills in novel ways as a part of the mechanics of play. In 24/7 the Game, students play number tiles one at a time on a game board grid. Players score points when the tile they placed creates one or more scoring conditions, which include sums of seven or twenty-four, sets, and runs. Similar to the many familiar word-building games that use this play mechanic, the challenge becomes finding ways to play as the board fills and tiles begin to intermingle. Adding to this challenge is a rule that does not allow a string of tiles to exceed the sum of twenty-four. When a set of tiles in any row, column, or diagonal reaches twenty-four, then two stones are placed on either end of the string, effectively removing those spaces from play. This game has students using math strategically as they plan, build, and react to the numbers on the board and in their hand. Success comes from having a flexible perspective, as each number placed can interact with other numbers in more than one direction. Students move beyond simply focusing on a single sum or set and must manage multiple mathematical expressions to find the most beneficial placement each turn.

Another mathematics-based game, 7 Ate 9, is a fast-playing card game that masks rote addition practice with a lot of fun. Players work at emptying their hands by playing cards based on the face-up card in the center of the table. Each card features its value predominantly in the center, with a plus and minus modifier in the corner. It is the application of the modifier that dictates which cards can be placed next. A five with ± two allows students to follow with either a three or a seven. In addition, the number range of the game is a closed set of one to ten. So if students need to add or subtract beyond those numbers, they simply need to carry around like they would on a clock. This is a game of free play, and the fun lies in its frantic pace as students race to play cards before their peers.

Tumblin-Dice is a dexterity game in which students take turns propelling dice from a plateau down a waterfall of steps. Each landing features a multiplier for the face value of the die, with the higher multipliers being on more difficult-to-reach areas. While scoring is featured heavily, it is the frequency and fun of scoring that make the game valuable. Students will not simply be tallying their score at the end but actively calculating throughout the game the possible combinations that would keep them in competition. While the game comes with six-sided dice, a higher-sided die can easily be used to vary the range of multipliers.

The last game of note is Numbers League, a game of basic math, superhero style. Students construct superheroes from cards with varying positive, negative, whole, and decimal values. The sum of those values is the hero's power, which is used, alone or in combination with other heroes, to capture the villains. Each villain has a value that needs to be matched in order to be captured. How that value is reached is completely open, so students are continually looking for ways to combine their superheroes to reach those values. Also at their disposal are one-use modifiers that may add to, take away from, or multiply a hero's value. The possible combinations will have students actively drawing on a whole range of math skills as they seek to wield justice.

Probability

Many games feature some element of probability, where students weigh their choices against the chances that certain events may or may not happen. While probability may factor to some degree in many decisions made, it is when there are a fixed number of known variables in the game that it becomes most beneficial. Incan Gold is a fine example of a push-your-luck game that demonstrates the value of probability. In the game, fifteen treasure and fifteen danger cards are shuffled to create a deck of encounters for an ancient ruin. Students go room to room, searching for treasure and hoping to avoid dangers. Before moving forward to a new room, players must decide if they want to leave with what treasures they have or risk going forward. If the student knows how many of each type of card are left in the deck, he can use probability to help influence his decisions based on what has already been encountered.

Number Sense and Value

Learning to understand the value of numbers and how they relate to each other is an early and important step in math literacy. Students need opportunities to learn that there are multiple avenues to a single number value. Double Shutter, a variation on the classic dice game of Shut the Box, gets students thinking about combination possibilities. Students take turns rolling dice as many times as they can, flipping down numbers in a box. There are two rows of the numbers one to nine situated one in front of the other. Players roll a pair of dice and flip down any combination of numbers that add up to the value of the roll. As numbers in the front row are flipped down, they provide access to those in the back. Game play, while fast and simple, reminds students that there are multiple ways to reach a number value.

Progressing from understanding the value of a single number is understanding how those values relate to each other. Number Chase is a game of mathematical deduction using number sense and value as players try to guess a secret number using a series of clues. Each clue helps students narrow down the choices by providing insight into the number's value and placement. Is it larger than twenty? Does it fall in a range of numbers or have a three in it? These and other questions give students the information needed to apply reasoning and logic toward finding the secret number.

Like any subject, mathematics benefits from differentiated instruction. Our goal as educators is to connect students with knowledge to help them grow as learners. Math requires practice as students work toward mastery, but without variety it can be difficult to maintain focus. By supplementing learning activities with games that address the same math content, teachers and librarians can create a rich assortment of learning experiences for students.

SCIENCE

Games can be a fun and engaging way to introduce or reinforce elements of the science curriculum. Most often this is accomplished through game mechanics, where elements of different schools of science and technology are used as a part of the learning experience. Because science lessons can benefit from hands-on experience, games are a prudent choice for classroom use. They allow students to interact with scientific theory and principles in a way that will make the content more meaningful and memorable.

Physics

The science of mass, matter, and its motion, physics is one of the most utilized in designer games. PitchCar and Crokinole are similar games that incorporate the concepts of friction, momentum, and angles as student flick disks within a playing area. Crokinole has been around for over a hundred years. It originated in Canada and features a round or hexagonal playing surface with scoring areas into which students try to get their disks. Similar to shuffleboard and curling, players can calculate the needed angles to remove their opponent's pieces while securing their own scoring positions. PitchCar overlays a car racing theme over the same mechanic, with students flicking their car disks around a wooden track.

Rails provide opportunities for angle and momentum calculation as students can bank or ride along them. Expansions for the base game include jumps, tunnels, and materials to construct a second level.

Progressing past simple applications of momentum and friction, games can approach the awe-inspiring exploration of gravity and the center of mass. Hamsterrolle features a narrow cylinder, segmented with shelves placed on the inside at regular intervals. Each student has a set of wooden shapes that she must get rid of by placing them farther along the cylinder than the last played piece. As more pieces are played, the cylinder rotates and raises the pieces already in play. Any pieces that fall are picked up by the player.

Bausack and Bamboleo are very similar games that push the boundaries of physics to the point of illusion. Bausack is simply a bag of blocks ranging from common to very unusual shapes. Students take turns selecting shapes for other players to add to their structure. Each player has a number of beans that they can pay with to pass on more challenging pieces. Players continue playing, building their structures up and hoping to be the last one standing. Bamboleo takes these pieces and places them on a platter with a cork ball on the bottom, which is balanced atop a conical stand. In contrast to Bausack's constructive use of the blocks, Bamboleo has students taking pieces away from the platter. As pieces are taken away, the platter's center shifts, causing some very interesting readjustments to the game. In both games, all of the situations that may arise, no matter how unbelievable, are explainable by the laws of physics. It is the exaggeration of circumstances created by unbelievable buildings or balancing acts that allows for animated dialogue surrounding these basic principles.

A less glamorous but more elegant application of physics is present in the racing game Bolide. In this realistic racing simulation, students make their way around the track using a vector-based movement system that highlights the effects of momentum. While not as awe-inspiring as other physics games, Bolide's strength lies in its strong connection to the curricular concepts of vectors and momentum.

Magnetism

Games can allow younger students to interact with scientific properties without needing to understand them. These early explorations provide a base that can be built upon later when the topic is covered as part of the classroom curriculum. Shiver-Stone Castle (Schloss Schlotterstein) features a nine-room castle raised on wooden legs in which students must guide a ghost to haunt different inhabitants. Each room is filled with a myriad of critters and creatures, making the location of the student's objective a mixture of memory and Where's Waldo? To move the ghost through the castle, students slide a long mallet with a magnet embedded in one end along the underside of the game board. Inside the bottom of the ghost is another magnet, and the combination of fields is strong enough that they attract each other through the game box. The basic game has students taking turns moving the ghost through the castle, trying to find a specific resident before time runs out. Game variations include Olympic-inspired events that use the principles of magnetism.

For slightly older students, Polarity illustrates the effects that multiple fields have on each other when they are introduced as well as how conditions change as field strengths are increased. A two-player game, Polarity has students take turns placing magnetized disks within the play area. In order to play a disk, it must be balanced at an angle off of one of the player's other disks. The more magnets that are placed, the more fields are in play. As the game progresses, the whole board becomes sensitive to the introduction of new fields and soon players' pieces become stacked, creating much stronger fields. Players score points for stacks in their color, and the game ends when one player has emptied their supply.

Environmental Science

It is imperative that students understand the impact that our actions have on the global environment. At a younger level, Arthur Saves the Planet: One Step at a Time gives students an opportunity to improve environmental concerns affecting Arthur's neighborhood. Students are working to collect the resources necessary to affect change. The game can be played either competitively or cooperatively, and it demonstrates the proximity of these issues as it seeks to motivate students into action by including specific examples of steps that can be taken in real life for each of the issues.

At the high school level, Power Grid is a game about energy choices and ethics as students build different types of plants to power cities. While the game doesn't address the polluting effects of the different types, it does illustrate the underlying financial motivations for resource choices. Students seek to expand their company and increase profits by maximizing their potential power output based on the availability of plants and resources on the market. Players quickly realize that while energy derived from renewable resources is ethically more sound, it can often be fiscally irresponsible depending on the resources available on the free market. This raises some interesting ethical debates regarding finance and the environment.

Scientific Method

While none of the games discussed directly teach the scientific method, many aspects of designer games help students develop and strengthen elements within the process. Inquiry is at the heart of the scientific method and is something students continually engage in throughout the game experience. Each turn, students examine the information available and, comparing it to the rules of play, ask themselves critical questions that directly affect the outcome of the game. Which action should I take? What value do I place on this? How much value does this hold for others? These, and other questions, influence the decisions of each player. Looking over a longer time scale, repeated plays of the same game are imperfect experiments where students are testing different strategy hypotheses, seeking the best approach to reach the desired outcome of victory.

Some games focus on specific aspects of inquiry. Suitcase Detectives and LetterFlip are two examples of games that require the application of deduction to be successful. In LetterFlip, students attempt to correctly guess the concealed words being held by the other player. Using their knowledge of vocabulary and word structure, students use a combination of deduction and luck to find the correct answers. A great game for the primary and elementary levels, Suitcase Detectives features a more pure use of deduction, as students attempt to ascertain which items have been stolen from the suitcase by comparing the shapes and outlines they can observe to the cards in their hands. Because the shapes overlap and are difficult to make out at times, students start with what they know is still in the suitcase and dismiss those items from consideration. The next progression is to look for parts of shapes that might help distinguish what else is still inside. By carefully narrowing down the options, young students are able to deduce which items have been stolen by a process of elimination.

All of these are just examples of how game play helps students develop a scientific mind-set. Games promote curiosity, inquiry, and reflection. Players repeat and refine their actions and choices as they work their way toward achieving their goals. Replacing a few words makes it even clearer: Science promotes curiosity, inquiry, and reflection. Scientists repeat and refine their actions and choices as they work their way toward achieving their goals.

PART III
Games in School Libraries

n the previous two sections, we have explored the theories behind the use of designer board games in school libraries through an exploration of the games and their connections to the curriculum. This section is devoted to the implementation of these ideas in the real world of school libraries. We will look at the model that has been successful in our region, talk about why we think it is especially well suited for replication in other libraries, and examine some of the challenges and questions surrounding implementation.

The Genesee Valley Model

The School Library System (SLS) of Genesee Valley BOCES provides support and services to the school libraries of twenty-two small, rural districts in western New York. For us, being part of a small organization has actually led to expanded opportunities for innovation and exploration. Though we came to librarianship through different paths, both of us share a long-time love of gaming. Despite a desire to bring games to school libraries, we had to wait to develop a program until we found a way to gain acceptance from the administrations in our member districts. The path forward combined Brian's connections to the curriculum through his school library experience with Christopher's administrative perspective. Instead of approaching gaming through individual librarians, we developed a top-down approach that sought acceptance and schoolwide adoption from principals and superintendents through the introduction of games as curriculum-aligned instructional resources that school libraries could use to promote student achievement.

The result has been a library of designer board games available to the school libraries in the districts of the Genesee Valley BOCES region. These games, while providing authentic fun and engagement, also address local, state, and national curriculum standards across many content areas including ELA, math, science, social studies, as well as twenty-first-century learning skills, as seen in the previous section. Our model has been incredibly successful because of three key elements: a low cost, a high level of buy-in, and a selection of games that are truly fun to play. None of these elements are unique to our region, and all should prove highly replicable in other situations.

LOW COST

One of the key ingredients for innovation and flexibility is a low price tag. This is one of the primary reasons why we decided to start our game collection with designer board and card games instead of video games. By doing so, our SLS was able to start a game library in 2007 with an initial investment of five hundred dollars, which went entirely to content. Unlike with a video game system where the console alone costs upward of two hundred and fifty dollars, there was no need to purchase expensive hardware or accessories. An average cost of about thirty dollars for a game as compared to higher costs for video games also allowed us to explore many different types of games to meet K–12 needs. Though it may seem like a small matter, consider this from an administrative perspective. The lower cost for board games leads to greater variety; in other words, the diversification of the investment reaches a wider audience and provides more opportunities for a positive return of student achievement. Additionally, requests for money are more flexible because orders can be adjusted to meet available funds without the need to cover a start-up cost for hardware.

For us, the five-hundred-dollar initial investment was a calculated risk. We wanted to start a program, and this seed money gave us an opportunity to test our ideas. Despite careful research, some of the first games we purchased turned out not to be the best selections. Most of the games, however, were wildly successful and helped us secure additional funding. As our library continues to grow, we have adopted a two-step purchasing process for most new games. In the first round, we evaluate regional curricular needs and research games that might provide a match. We then purchase single copies of the games we would like to consider adding to the collection. This lets us try the game in a real classroom environment before making a final selection. In the second round, we then purchase multiple copies of games that prove successful. We are buying for regional loans, but even in a single building it can help to have multiple copies of games to allow simultaneous play by a whole class. Because additional games can be purchased without the need for additional console hardware, this is a very cost-effective investment.

HIGH LEVEL OF BUY-IN

Our game program is by no means the first use of games in schools or school libraries, but it does seem to be unique in having a top-down approach to the adoption of gaming in schools. We have enjoyed great support from member librarians and teachers who see the success of the games with students, but we have also had a high level of support from school administrators and boards of education. As the demands of high-stakes testing eliminate art, music, and even recess from the school day, a program designed to bring games to the classroom might be expected to have a hard time gaining traction. By focusing on designer board and card games as curriculum-aligned instructional resources, however, our program becomes a natural fit for school library collections and classroom use.

To further support our gaming program we have also described our efforts in relation to research on gaming and learning. Though much of the research looks at video games, it can be generalized to the broader gaming experience in most cases. The writings of James Paul Gee (*What Video Games Have to Teach Us about Learning and Literacy,* 2007), Steven Johnson (*Everything Bad Is Good for You,* 2006), and John Beck (*Got Game,* 2004) have been excellent resources for talking to teachers and administrators about the ideas behind gaming. Being able to speak about gaming as it relates to learning theories has allowed us to connect with instructional leaders in schools. We are speaking their language—the language of curriculum and performance indicators. As a result, after only just over a year, our game collection is seeing a high level of usage from administrator-initiated workshops and demonstrations.

Spreading the message through principals and other instructional leaders combined with our focus on libraries has also made the process of getting games into schools more efficient. Instead of trying to justify the use of gaming in a single classroom, we are able to talk about the use of games as instructional resources with whole facilities. When we go into a school to work with a librarian, we often bring games out to show to a whole department. Whether in a similar regional setting or in a single district or school, building a gaming program out from libraries provides a central hub for resource collection and training.

SELECTION OF GAMES

Finally, our game library works because we are using authentic board games that were designed for gamers, not teachers. As discussed earlier, these are not "educational games," but rather complex games built for fun that have been carefully selected for their links to learning objectives. By engaging students within a quality play experience, we are able to demand a higher level of rigor in their tasks; they want to keep playing to win the game, so they are more willing to do the work. Though these games have been aligned with local, state, and national curriculum standards, this alignment is secondary to the quality of game play.

Teachers often ask us for games to meet a particular curriculum objective. In some cases, we are able to help; there are great games about the electoral process (1960: The Making of the President), vector motion (Bolide), and Cartesian coordinates (Oregon). When asked for games about grammar, though, we are unable to help. Unlike the natural tension of an election, or the use of map coordinates to claim land, grammar just does not lend itself to inclusion in a game as either a theme or a mechanic.

There are educational games about grammar, but in our experience they lack authentic game play and are no real fun; they are just worksheets with a spinner or some dice. Libraries that try to offer educational games as real games will find it very difficult to build student support.

MISSING PIECES

There are two questions we can always count on being asked when we talk about our model for a game library: the first is the length of time for which we loan the games, and the second is how we keep track of all the pieces from the games. Being a school library system that is building a game library for twenty-two member school districts with around sixty-five libraries means we approach the collection and loaning of games in a different way than a school or public library might. Our games are only loaned to member librarians, although they then distribute the games in their schools for use by teachers and students. The games are not yet available for direct loaning to students for home use. The loan period varies depending on the game, but our default loan is two weeks.

By loaning to member librarians, we also avoid some of the hassles of tracking pieces. We include inventory sheets inside the game boxes and expect our member librarians to check the contents of the game box before returning it. Most instruction sheets in the games include a detailed inventory so you do not have to count all the pieces to create your own sheet. There have not yet been any serious problems with missing pieces, but we are prepared for the eventual loss of something. Most game publishers that we have spoken to about this concern have been very helpful. Alan Moon's Ticket to Ride uses small plastic trains to claim routes across the United States. The number of trains is important as it determines the end of the game; in some games, the number of counter pieces is not as important, but in this game a missing train of a certain color would change the game for one player. The publisher, Days of Wonder, sells single replacement trains on their website, but they sent us a bag of about one hundred trains of each color to make sure our collection would be ready for any losses.

In other situations, games that turn up with missing items will be saved to supply spare parts to complete other games. After more than a year of use, one of our four copies of Numbers League lost a single card (out of hundreds of cards). That copy of the game was simply removed from circulation and added to the spare parts drawer. Unlike books with missing pages or puzzles with missing pieces, games are very easily made whole. In this case, Numbers League can easily withstand the loss of a single villain card out of over forty villain cards with no real loss in playability. If the game were not typically used in a whole-class setting where the missing card makes one game setup slightly different, the missing card would not even be noticeable. In other cases, missing markers or pieces can be replaced with generic colored wooden cubes or other replacements. Wooden markers of various colors, shapes, and sizes are readily available to fill in as needed if game publishers cannot supply extra pieces to cover losses.

We have found, however, that most publishers of designer board games are very willing to work with libraries to find solutions to potential problems. In most cases, they had never thought about the implications for their games being used either in libraries or as a lending collection in a library. In libraries, we are familiar with the idea of special library bindings that help books withstand the higher level of use. Designer board games could also be published in library versions with built-in compensation for loss of pieces through inclusion of additional pieces or use of more generic markers that could be used interchangeably with a number of different games.

USING THE GAMES

With fears of missing pieces laid to rest, the next big challenge is figuring out how to actually use games in school libraries. We have come up with a comprehensive plan for getting the games from the School Library System of Genesee Valley BOCES into the libraries and classrooms of the region. There are two major parts: how game use is initiated and when the games are used. For many libraries and schools, the use of games is a new concept, and a high level of professional development and support is necessary. Our system provides that support through what are best described as push-in and pull-out development activities. Our professional conversations with librarians also establish a framework for appropriate times and types of game use.

As a regional system with a game library, we are able to provide a high level of support and professional development for our member libraries. As part of the School Improvement division of our organization, we are charged with delivering a large part of our regular professional development as direct support in our member libraries. To accomplish this, we push-in to libraries and provide coteaching along with librarians and classroom teachers in order to model the use of games for instruction. This has proven to be an incredibly effective way to introduce games to students and teachers for the first time. Librarians and teachers are put at ease by the presence of a game expert who can teach the mechanics of play. From our perspective, even more important than the mechanics is the expertise we can provide in modifications to games to make them better for classroom use.

So what does this look like in practice? In one case, the two of us took 1960: The Making of the President into a high school library for use with senior social studies classes. The librarian set up the program with the classroom teacher as a culminating activity for a study of elections; the lesson took place in the library because of the large tables required for the oversize board in 1960. For the first couple of classes, we taught the game. Throughout the day, though, the librarian and teacher stepped up to take over instruction. Teaching a class how to play a game can be a challenge; 1960 is a very complicated game, and delivery of full instructions on game play would extend well beyond the attention span of the class. Instead, it is often best to give just enough instruction to get things going. Additional rules and procedures can be addressed at the point of need in game play. The most critical elements to address in the introduction of a game include the point of the game (the backstory or thematic elements that describe why you doing things in the game), a quick review of the pieces, and how to start the first turn. We like to use presentation software to show classes pictures of the pieces and provide a quick overview of turns. Document cameras can also be an effective way to share a game with a larger group.

To make it easier to get through the first turn of 1960 in a short period, we used another game instruction trick. Each of the game boards was set up so that the teams would have the same cards in their first hand. This meant we would be able to talk about the different types of cards we had selected and begin to identify strategies arising from the interactions of those cards. Preset scenarios can be a very effective instructional tool even after the initial introduction of a game. By setting up a certain environment, teachers and librarians can focus on a particular concept or idea. Given a set of superheroes and tools in Chris Pallace's Numbers League, what combinations can be used to capture either the most or the highest value of numeric villains? In historical games, preset scenarios can be used to either simulate history or provide an opportunity to reevaluate a critical moment in our past. Here I Stand, an incredibly ambitious game by Ed Beach that addresses the Wars of the Reformation (1517–1555), even includes an extra book that details turn-by-turn card play that demonstrates the actual path of history. This level of detail makes the game an incredible resource for school libraries to provide, but, like 1960: The Making of the President, the complexity of the game introduces the challenge of fitting a long game into short periods.

With forty-five-minute periods, we often have to modify games to facilitate extension through multiple class sessions. In the case of 1960, we accomplished this by creating a sheet that lets students record their current status so they can set up the board again later. This simple sheet features a map of the United States for recording the number of cubes in each state along with extra spaces for recording the other details of game play. This is in no way a perfect solution, as there is no easy way to record the status of the deck and cards that have been played; this method assumes that the entire deck will be reshuffled each game. If the point of using 1960 in a library or classroom is to provide an immersive experience related to the electoral process, however, then the issue of the cards is a minor problem that does not affect the desired learning. It might also be possible to contact the publisher, Z-Man Games, to purchase additional decks of cards for 1960 so that each group could have their own deck.

Another strategy for handling longer games is to highlight their length instead of trying to compensate for it. An eight-hour game like Here I Stand can be a featured part of a longer unit of instruction by making it larger than a board game. Post the game board on a bulletin board and focus on turn-by-turn play over a number of weeks. Instead of individuals, whole classes could take on each of the six roles in the game to turn this into a much bigger game experience. Many other board games can benefit from this hyperenlargement; even traditional games like chess take on a new feeling when played on giant outside boards. Game conferences often feature life-size re-creations of popular board games played out in large spaces. This often requires more thought and imagination than resources. For example, the hallways of a school with square floor tiles can be turned into a giant racetrack for Alfredo Genovese's Bolide. This game uses vector-based movement defined by movement through the intersections of a square grid pattern. The only pieces would be students (as the cars) and a marker to show momentum. As effective as Bolide is for demonstrating vectors and momentum, making the students stand in for the cars in a Bolide-inspired race would make the learning even more concrete.

Use of games in school libraries also extends beyond the classroom. With a collection of authentic games, curriculum alignments can be set aside to let the playability of the game shine through. Many of the librarians in the Genesee Valley BOCES region borrow games not only for instructional use, but also to make available during study halls or library class checkout times. What the students don't realize is that by playing these quality designer games during study time in the library, they are still practicing their information skills. Many of the games in our collection align to a specific classroom content area, but all of them align with the American Association of School Librarians Standards for the 21st-Century Learner. The games all require critical thinking and information processing during game play, even if the students just think they are provided for enjoyment.

PROFESSIONAL DEVELOPMENT

Librarians also come to workshops we provide to learn how to play a variety of games that they can then implement independently. Running a library gaming workshop is similar to a technology workshop. In many cases, the audience is unfamiliar with the concepts being addressed. As such, it is important to provide a two-prong approach that addresses an explanation of the purpose of games while also giving participants time for hands-on practice with the games In our experience, the biggest challenge is getting participants in the door; once they see what designer board games have to offer, they are sold. Even though we always make sure to talk about designer board games as curriculum-aligned instructional resources, most workshop participants simply have no frame of reference for these games. In their mind, board games refer to either traditional American board games with little instructional value or educational products masquerading as games.

Librarians and teachers often come to game workshops unsure about what to expect. If the workshop facilitator can quickly immerse participants in a gaming experience, it helps establish an environment that mixes play and learning. Some effective games for starting workshops are Werewolf and Incan Gold. Both of these games are easy to teach and scale well from small groups to large groups with only a single copy needed.

There are many versions of Werewolf available from publishers, though the editions from Ted Alspach (Ultimate Werewolf: Ultimate Edition) and Dimitry Davidoff (Werewolves of Miller's Hollow) provide nice editions with comprehensive rules. The basic rules are quite simple and can easily be found online; the cards for player roles can be anything, even just scraps of paper. The game is essentially an interactive storytelling experience guided by the moderator. The boxed versions provide helpful hints for running a successful game. School librarians will want to be sure to modify the game as needed to meet age appropriateness. In the original game, werewolves kill villagers every night and one person is accused and killed every day until the werewolves are discovered or the village is decimated. In our school uses, we talk about villagers being kidnapped and the accused being arrested and taken away.

Another nice introductory game is Alan Moon and Bruno Faidutti's Incan Gold. This game presents a nice mixture of English and language arts from storytelling along with math in the disbursement of treasure encountered during exploration. Like Werewolf, Incan Gold needs a strong facilitator to create drama as the game moves through the Incan ruins encountering dangers. The game itself works best with about six players, but it is quite easy to run multiple games in a workshop by breaking participants up into groups of the right size. Each group can then work from the same set of cards revealed and described by the facilitator by keeping track of individual progress on a scoring sheet completed by each group to note when people leave and what treasures are left behind in each room. Either of these games provides a great opportunity to focus discussion on the ideas of curriculum alignment, content skills used in game play, and how players interacted within the game. Once participants are in a game-playing frame of mind, it is much easier to introduce other games and talk about how they can be used in libraries and classrooms.

When introducing games, it is important that the presenter be familiar with the games. Think of this as doing a booktalk for the games; you could never booktalk something you hadn't read. As complex resources aligned through both the theme and the mechanics, games require extra attention to unlock their full potential. When talking about games, it helps to identify the best grade/age range, the ideal number of players and/or teams, the length of time it will really take to play, and the extent of curriculum alignment. It also helps librarians and teachers better visualize how they could use the game if the presenter can share tips for classroom use. Does the game scale well for team play? Can it be modified for use over multiple periods? Though some of this information may be available, in most cases you will need to play the game to learn how it works.

Playing games is the real key to professional development about games in libraries. Because designer board games are so foreign to most librarians, it is critical that they receive hands-on experience with the games in a friendly and helpful environment. Again, as with technology, it is probably best not to just throw the participants in to struggle with learning the games on their own. Some of the designer games can be complicated for those who lack understanding of the basic common mechanics. Additionally, the included rules and directions are often translated into English and may not be as clear as needed. In most cases, a facilitator can more quickly and effectively describe a game. Just like with technology workshops, don't be afraid to call upon student experts as workshop helpers to have enough facilitators to explain all the games.

Starting a Game
Collection

T he hope is that at this point in the book you are ready to consider starting a collection of designer board games in your school library. Game collections start like any other set of library resources, with careful consideration and selection of materials for inclusion. Though games may seem different, school librarians regularly make professional judgment calls on the selection of other resource types like videos, websites, and audio programs. It must be stressed that games need to be viewed as any other type of resource in a school library.

COLLECTION DEVELOPMENT

Careful selection of games is a critical part of creating a successful program. School libraries should already have an established selection policy approved by the board of education or other local school governance body. If your policy is modeled on the sample presented in the American Library Association's Workbook for Selection Policy Writing, it most likely already supports the purchase of games as learning resources. (Games are included in the extensive list of resource types presented under Objectives of Selection in the first part of the policy.) That sample policy also provides general guidance for evaluation of materials that can be applied to the selection of games. In formalizing the selection procedures for the Game Library of the School Library System of Genesee Valley BOCES, four criteria for evaluation were established.

AUTHENTICITY OF GAME PLAY

Just as librarians seek good books, they also need to seek good games. We were not looking for the traditional "educational games" found in many school catalogs. Too often they fail to engage students in an enjoyable game experience; just as with bad books, students see right through bad games. Instead, we look for games that gamers play. Many designer board games already include elements that can be aligned to curriculum standards. The inclusion is not always intentional, but rather a natural result of a well-designed game that uses a rich theme and complex mechanics.

Amun-Re was not designed by Reiner Knizia to be an educational game about Egypt. In his typical fashion, Knizia designed an intricate auction game that pushes players to interact in a careful dance of give-and-take. By combining multiple types of both hidden and open auctions, Amun-Re forces middle school students to consider their opponents in a different way. This very authentic game, however, also happens to provide a powerful introduction to ancient Egypt. While playing the game, students are using vocabulary and encountering ideas such as the separation of Old and New Kingdoms and the importance of the river Nile. As a librarian, your collection development challenge is to find these authentic games that address curriculum standards, as opposed to settling for the prepackaged educational games that sound good in a catalog but fail to engage students.

In the quest for a good game, however, it is important to remember that good can easily be mistaken for a subjective adjective. Just like with any other library resource, it is important to try and approach games with an objective eye. Like less favored genres of fiction, there will be types of game mechanics that you don't enjoy. The key is to try the games with students or other players to see how they interact with the games. The definition that we use for a good game draws heavily on the characteristics of the European-style board games: We are looking for a complex game mechanic that challenges students to engage in critical thinking, although we are less enamored of those games that use speed to define a winner of a critical thinking challenge. Games where users remain in the game working toward a set of victory conditions are preferred over elimination-style games. We also place a high importance on the replay value of the game; variable board setups or multiple paths to victory help keep games interesting over time. Finally, while these other factors can be evaluated, it can be more difficult to quantify fun. Fun—the real measure of an authentically good game—can perhaps be defined as the desire of students to engage (repeatedly) in the challenging game play. Once the level of fun is determined, then it is time to see if the game is appropriate for inclusion in a school library collection.

IDENTIFICATION OF CURRICULUM ALIGNMENTS

Our collection development focuses on alignment with the American Association of School Librarians (AASL) Standards for the 21st-Century

Learner and the New York State Learning Standards. By completing these alignments and documenting the ways in which the designer games in our collection support learning, we are better able to justify gaming as a part of classroom learning. Curriculum alignment is basically the practice of looking at the curriculum standards and then evaluating resources to see which of the standards are addressed by use of specific resources. The alignment process often begins with consideration of the broad standards themselves, but it should never end at that level. Curriculum standards are intentionally large statements that encompass a great deal of knowledge for the purposes of categorization. For example, the AASL Standards for the 21st-Century Learner condense everything that a K–12 student needs to learn about information literacy into four standards statements. While alignment to these broad statements can help clarify the overall concept of a game as being about critical thinking as opposed to creation of new understandings, it becomes much less useful in other content areas. For that reason, it is important to go down to a deeper level of the curriculum document, performance indicators.

Performance indicators should be distinct statements that identify a single learning objective that students are expected to master and be able to perform. For example, a larger math standard might talk about computation, but a performance indicator would specify that students need to be able to add two numbers or multiply numbers with decimals. Given those performance indicators, it is possible to look at a game like Chris Pallace's Numbers League to see whether it requires demonstration of mastery of the skills listed in the performance indicators. In Numbers League, players construct superheroes from numerical heads, bodies, and legs. For example, a four head could combine with a two body and a three set of legs to create a superhero with a value of nine $(4 + 2 + 3 = 9)$. In order to use her superhero, a student will have to demonstrate mastery of the addition of three numbers. It can then be said that Numbers League is aligned with whatever math performance indicator addresses addition of three numbers.

Standards alignment is a big job, so it is most easily tackled over time as a regular part of learning and using the games in your collection. While playing a game like Amun-Re, for example, we are working on a metalevel to analyze how the game's theme and mechanics could support classroom use. In particular, we are looking for alignment to the performance indicators from local, state, and national curriculum standards. In the case of Amun-Re, there is a strong correlation with sixth grade and ninth grade social studies standards for New York State that address ancient civilizations. It must be stressed that these alignments should not be confused with direct instructional support materials. Amun-Re will not provide the same information about ancient Egypt that could be found in a reference source. The game encourages learning by establishing a level of prior knowledge, understanding, and application that may not be available from other sources. It establishes a frame of reference that can be called upon during later instruction: "Remember when we played Amun-Re and between the Old Kingdom turns and the New Kingdom turns, you lost control of your provinces and all the farmers went away but the pyramids stayed? Here is why that occurred in the game . . ."

GAME TIME

When collecting games for use in a school library, it is necessary to consider the length of time needed to set up, teach, play, and put away a game. More specifically, the time needed to play a game needs to be directly compared to the length of time in a period or block for your school. An ideal length of time for a middle or high school game seems to be about forty minutes; in an elementary or primary setting, most games should require no more than twenty minutes. While longer games are certainly considered—many of the games in our collection take an hour or two and one takes about eight hours—they require additional evaluation. There must be a way for a longer game to be broken into natural turns that can be completed during a single class period for completion over a series of days. Amun-Re includes a natural breaking point in the game representing the split between the Old and New Kingdoms. The game can be paused at that point or ended early and scored for just the first half. In some cases, very long games can be extended over an entire semester with a turn taken each week. For longer games, the fourth criterion becomes more important.

RETURN ON INVESTMENT

All games that we select, but longer or more complex games in particular, are evaluated to determine a potential return on investment. If a teacher is going to invest a week of class periods on a game, then it must be one of the best ways for students to learn a topic. On the other hand, games that are selected for casual play in a study hall with a low investment in setup and instruction can have a lower return. This culminating criterion really combines the other three points of evaluation into a single test to see if the game is worth adding to the collection. Additional consideration is given here to the complexity of game setup and takedown as well as other factors like the number of pieces. This is also the point at which you can stop to consider the potential impact of the game on learning. Is a game, and the game being considered in particular, the best way for a student to learn about the subject? Is it adding value to the students' understanding of certain aspects of the topic that cannot be addressed otherwise? Overall, this step is a final check to make sure that the game is the right game to be added to a school library collection.

When we selected Amun-Re for inclusion in our collection as a game addressing ancient Egypt, we also evaluated other games about ancient civilizations. One of the games, Martin Wallace's Perikles, addressed ancient Greece. Perikles is definitely an authentic game, it has a pretty strong alignment to the ninth grade curriculum, and although it takes a few hours to play, there are natural breaking points. The problem with Perikles is that it just doesn't provide a strong enough return on a very high investment. Even though it can be taught without too much trouble, the game is quite complicated. There are many pieces that have to be set up on the board, and a great deal of time is spent just moving bits around for each phase. Even though it does a great job of re-creating the political tensions and constant struggles between the Greek city-states, Perikles is just too much work. It is a wonderful game and we enjoyed playing it, but it does not provide a strong enough return on such a high investment and could not be included in our library collection.

WHERE TO FIND GAMES

By this point, the beneficial reasons for including modern board games in school libraries are so established that the primary question remaining is where to find these excellent games. Unfortunately, this is not the easiest question to answer. Despite their arguably superior game play, modern board games have struggled to break into the mainstream American market. Most of the games discussed in this book will not be available in general retail stores. Some of the titles can be found at independent book or toy stores, but in most cases a specialty game store will be required. Though there may be some initial difficulties in working out purchasing agreements, working with small game stores can end up being a huge benefit to a school library. Whether a local store or an online vendor, establishing a partnership with a game store gives a school library access to experts for questions or recommendations.

Local Game Stores

Game specialty stores can be interesting places. This book has focused on designer board and card games, but a visit to a game store will probably reveal the equally interesting worlds of role-playing systems, collectible card games, and miniatures gaming. While these might not be games that your library would use, knowing about these types of games is important for libraries; there are designer board games available that use similar mechanics that might be a beneficial addition to a collection. For example, Richard Borg's Memoir '44 provides a more accessible version of miniatures gaming built around important battles of World War II. Though there are expansion packs available that offer additional units and rules, the original game provides a nice introduction to the basic concepts of miniatures gaming. Players use action cards to deliver orders, move figures on the board, and then roll special dice for combat encounters. Social studies teachers can use this to provide a visual demonstration of how key battles progressed or offer students a chance to see if history can be rewritten. Working with a local game store can give a library an opportunity to explore possibilities.

There are other ways that libraries and game stores can work together. Like libraries, many of these small stores function as community gathering places for their customers. Stores will often provide tables for open game play as well as more formal tournaments, which are often sponsored by the game publishers. School or public libraries could work with game stores to have a presence at those tournaments that would draw school-age children. Additionally, game stores often have open copies of designer games for in-store play. School libraries could work with a game store

Role-Playing, Collectible Card, and Miniatures Games

Most role-playing games are sold as sets of rule books that create a world for the game. There is usually a game master who guides players as they work through adventures. Even if these are not part of your gaming program, libraries can still consider supporting role-playing by collecting some of the core rule books from different systems.

Collectible card games (CCGs) tend to be very popular among school-age children, as many of the games are based on popular animated television shows and manga imported from Japan. In this format, players buy packages of randomized cards attempting to collect sets of cards with different powers. From these cards, customized decks are built for game play. Though the games themselves would be difficult to add to a collection, libraries can still support these gamers by looking for graphic novels or other books from the same series.

Like CCGs, miniatures gaming includes building a collection of pieces. Miniatures may be drawn from a fantasy-themed world or may be used to re-create historic battles.

to see about hosting a game night in the school using the resources and expertise from the store.

Building a relationship with a local game store is also one of the best ways to purchase games for your school library. Game stores can work with distributors to order games as needed. In some cases, a school library order for a few hundred dollars may represent a significant portion of a store's weekly sales; therefore, the game store may be able to offer a discount on the order. When starting a business relationship with a game store, it will probably be necessary to discuss purchasing options. Game stores are often small businesses that may be run in a casual manner. Do not be surprised if the store doesn't know what a purchase order is or how to accept one. Even if they tell you that purchase orders are acceptable, make sure there is a clear understanding that the purchase order will represent the form of payment with actual funds being sent within a month after the purchase. If the store cannot accept a purchase order, school business offices can sometimes provide a check for the time of game delivery if the store writes a letter on letterhead stating that they do not accept purchase orders. The key here is communication, both with the store and with your business office.

Online Purchasing

The other option for purchasing designer board games is going through an online store. There are many online board game stores offering a wide variety of products with a range of price discounts. For schools and libraries, a good option is Funagain Games at http://funagain.com. Funagain is one of the only sites able to accept purchase orders from schools and libraries. Another way to purchase games online is to go through Amazon .com. Though Amazon itself does not have many designer board games, the affiliate store program can allow schools and libraries to purchase through an Amazon business account. Online stores will usually have a larger selection than a local store, and may even be able to offer a better price, but they cannot offer the same level of browsing and support that a local game store can provide.

PART IV
Great Games for School Libraries

Knowing how to start building a game collection can be intimidating. Even when armed with well-developed selection criteria, finding gaming resources that are effective at engaging students and addressing the curriculum requires an experienced eye.

To help you get started, this section features lists of ten recommended games for each of the elementary, middle, and high school levels. Each game included was professionally selected according to the selection criteria highlighted earlier, and each should provide an authentic gaming experience with a return on investment that makes it a worthwhile endeavor. Beyond this initial qualification, every title has been field-tested multiple times and has received positive feedback from students and educators on both its curricular and its engagement value.

Like any potential resource, the games on these lists should be judged based on the needs of your program. Whether used to strengthen existing lessons or to spark new collaborative endeavors, each of these games has the potential to have a positive impact on student achievement.

Top Recommended Games for Elementary School

Pre-K through Grade 5

Froggy Boogie
Published by: Blue Orange Games
Designed by: Thierry Denoual
Curricular area: Math
Year published: 2007
Number of players: 2–6
Playing time: 15 minutes

Used with permission from Blue Orange Games

A classically crafted game of memory and matching, Froggy Boogie challenges the youngest learners with simplicity tempered with quality. In the game, each student is trying to help their baby frog make its way around the pond without being seen by the adult frogs.

On their turn, players attempt to sneak their baby frogs forward one lily pad by rolling a set of colored dice. Each adult frog is multicolored with two large goggly eyes that can be lifted out. One eye features the image of a frog, which indicates the baby frog was seen, while the other is blank. Using the resulting color combination from the roll, students find the matching adult frog on the table and lift out one of the eyes. If they were seen, the turn ends and the next player takes her turn. If it is blank, she moves her baby frog forward one lily pad and rolls again. The first frog to make it around the pond is the winner.

Froggy Boogie provides an engaging resource for use as an enrichment activity in a math center or for larger groups; multiple copies can be used to engage the whole class. Through the game, students not only strengthen color recognition skills, they also begin to develop more complex strategies for organizing information as they develop ways to remember the right choice for each of the different color combinations on the table.

Gopher It!

Published by: Playroom Entertainment
Designed by: Reinhard Staupe
Curricular area: Math
Year published: 2003
Number of players: 2–4
Playing time: 10 minutes

Used with permission from Playroom Entertainment

Gopher It! marries risk management with basic addition skills to present some fun and challenging choices for beginning learners. In the game, students are gophers working to collect food for the coming winter. Each turn, players can draw up to four cards from the supply in the middle of the table. Featured on the cards are varying numbers of either apples, carrots, or nuts that players are trying to add to their stockpiles so that any one food type adds up to exactly six. When a player collects a total of six of a food type, they collect a trophy and clear their stockpile to start fresh.

While this is a seemingly simple task, there are several risks that each student must consider when drawing cards. If he draws the same food type twice in a row, he must stop and put back any food he drew this turn. Additionally, if one of his stockpile totals adds up to more than six, then he must put all of that food type back to the supply. Suddenly math becomes meaningful, as students begin to consider the implications of each pull from the supply pile, using addition as a guide for their actions.

This game succeeds on many levels. Apart from the math skills and simple mechanics, Gopher It! is able to introduce opportunities for critical thinking and self-assessment at a very young age. It makes an excellent choice for use as reinforcement for a small group of struggling students or as part of a math center.

In the Country

Published by: HABA—Habermaaß GmbH
Designed by: Markus Nikisch
Curricular area: Science
Year published: 2006
Number of players: 2–4
Playing time: 20 minutes

Used with permission from HABA—Habermaaß GmbH

On a farm, breakfast doesn't come from the supermarket but from the resources at hand. Bread is milled from grain, eggs come from chickens, and don't forget to milk the cows! Markus Nikisch's In the Country helps students familiarize themselves with the nutrition cycle and basic agriculture by providing the locale and the raw materials needed to make everyday foods.

In the game, students work on a country farm complete with cows, chickens, wheat fields, and a mill. Each player is working toward completing a recipe for her Grandma Edna's birthday. Some recipes are simple, while others are more complex and require goods to be processed before completion. As an example, to make an apple pie, students need to gather apples, milk (by feeding hay to the cows), flour (by taking wheat to the mill), and eggs (by feeding grain to the chickens). This process is made very accessible through the use of pictures on the recipe cards, so students can focus on planning their actions rather than trying to remember what they need.

The mechanics of play are simple: On a player's turn they roll two dice; one die will show an animal and the other a number. Each student uses the numbered dice to move around the farm and collect the resources she needs by laying tractor tokens down end to end from her starting position and placing her farmer at the end. If the farmer is touching a resource she needs, she gets to take it.

In the Country is a hearty handful for young players. The high-quality components will captivate the imagination, while the game play will strengthen vital concepts and skills such as cause and effect, sequencing, planning, and spatial awareness. The game can be played both competitively or cooperatively. Cooperative play can allow for more students to be involved, but the need to strategically maneuver the farmers around the board will cap the number in the single digits. This game's short game time makes it an excellent activity for small groups, perhaps as part of a learning center or as an enrichment activity for students finished with work.

Incan Gold

Published by: FRED Distribution
Designed by: Alan R. Moon and
Bruno Faidutti
Curricular area: Math
Year published: 2006
Number of players: 3–8
Playing time: 20 minutes

Used with permission from FRED Distribution

Incan Gold gives students the opportunity to press their luck in search of treasure as they explore ancient ruins in the jungles of Peru. Along the way, they will have to draw on their understanding of probability and division if they hope to come away with any of the lost riches. Play revolves around a deck of thirty cards that includes fifteen hazard cards (three each of five different dangers) and fifteen treasure cards. These cards serve as the rooms of the ruin, with both benefit and peril possible behind every door. Each turn, before a card is revealed, players must decide whether they continue forward or turn back to camp with whatever treasure they have already collected. Those who continue forward must resolve whatever appears in the next room. Treasure is divided equally among the players, with any left over remaining in the room. Encountered hazards serve as a warning the first time they appear and the end to the expedition the second. Players who choose to return to camp not only keep any treasure they have found, they get the added benefit of collecting any treasure left behind—if it can be divided equally among those who chose to leave at that point as well.

Incan Gold is a great large-group or whole-class learning experience. Because the game scales well up to eight players, two or three copies should accommodate a whole classroom. When using the game with a class, one alternative to traditional play is to have students break into expedition groups but have the school librarian or teacher lead the expedition with only one set of cards used for everybody. Each expedition group would divide the treasures and weigh the probabilities concurrently with, but independently from, the others, with a winner emerging from each group.

Max

Published by: Family Pastimes, Ltd.
Designed by: Jim Deacove
Curricular areas: ELA and social studies
Year published: 1986
Number of players: 1–8
Playing time: 20 minutes

Used with permission from Family Pastimes Ltd.

The first years of school are full of exploration and discovery when, among other things, students start laying foundations for the social skills that will carry them through their school years and beyond. Games like Jim Deacove's Max can provide a social playground for developing interaction and engagement skills.

Max is a cooperative game for early elementary students that rewards discussion and cooperation. In the game, players work together to help a group of neighborhood critters get safely back home to their tree while avoiding Max the neighborhood cat.

On the surface, Max appears to be a simple roll-and-move game, but the very first turn reveals deeper decisions. Rather than numbers, each die face features either a black or green pip. Green pips allow the player to move one of the critters forward a space, while black pips move Max. If players approach the game competitively by "adopting" a critter and only working to save that one, they will soon find that Max has caught up with them all. The other alternative to rolling is using a "treat" to call Max back to the house, giving the players a reprieve from the hunt.

Max is a simple game with very interesting decisions to be made. Students need to continually assess the current situation and make tough choices: to roll or to use their turn to call Max back, to move one critter twice or two critters once. While the artwork may come across as a little dated, the theme and complexity level are a perfect match with young students. Because of the potential for dialogue, Max is easily expandable beyond the recommended player limit. Two copies can easily engage a classroom of students, while a single copy can provide an excellent activity for a small group of students. However it is used, Max is sure to help young learners see the strengths of a cooperative approach to solving problems.

Number Chase
Published by: Playroom Entertainment
Designed by: Reinhard Staupe
Curricular area: Math
Year published: 2006
Number of players: 2–5
Playing time: 15 minutes

Used with permission from Playroom Entertainment

Reinhard Staupe's Number Chase engages students with the mathematical concepts of number sense, range, and inequality in a quick and enjoyable learning experience. The game consists of a set of fifty numbered cards that are laid out in sequential order. To start, one player secretly selects one of the numbers; each of the other players takes turns trying to guess that number based on the information they have available.

Initially the students have nothing but luck to work from, but as the game progresses, each unsuccessful guess provides more information as the card is flipped over to reveal a question on the opposite side. Players can learn a variety of information, including whether the number is odd or even, is between a range of numbers, or is greater or less than a particular number. The player who selected the number must truthfully answer each question, providing additional pieces of information that can be applied to any of the remaining choices.

Through deduction and inquiry, students are able to successfully work their way to the correct answer. Along the way, they will need to draw upon their knowledge of mathematics to help them reach their goal.

While the game rules describe play with up to five people, the game is easily playable with an entire class of students. One possible scenario is round robin play, with one student selecting a number and the rest of the class taking turns trying to guess the correct answer. When a student is successful, the next in line selects a new number and the game continues. With the short time and accessibility of the game, this makes Number Chase an excellent choice for elementary school libraries.

Quiddler

Published by: Set Enterprises, Inc.
Designed by: Marsha Falco
Curricular area: ELA
Year published: 1998
Number of players: 1–8
Playing time: 30 minutes

Word building and phonemic awareness are the centerpiece of this fast and familiar card game where students use letters and blends to build rummy-style melds in their hand. As play progresses, Quiddler rewards word exploration as students build and test their vocabulary while they accumulate points in a progression of card hands.

The game itself is very easy to set up and teach. Students are dealt a hand of cards with any remaining cards creating a draw pile. The top card from the draw pile is flipped to start a discard pile and the play is off. On her turn, a student draws a card and tries to arrange her hand into words made from a combination of two or more cards. If she can use all the cards from her hand, minus a discard, then she is able to go out. Each remaining player gets one last chance to draw and play cards from his hand before scoring for the round.

What makes Quiddler such a good choice for learning environments is the game's inclusiveness. Through a blend of mechanics and scoring, students of all skill levels can successfully interact and engage in the same play experience. Beginning and struggling spellers work to reinforce their high-frequency words, building mastery over these cornerstones of language, while more sophisticated spellers are able to push themselves to build longer, more challenging words. Students can also further their vocabulary by using a dictionary while play moves around the table to find words they can make from the cards in their hand.

While the game calls for eight hands to be played, it can easily be modified to fit into a smaller chunk of time or played over the course of several days. Another option is to use several copies of the game to create tournament play, with students vying to become the Quiddler King or Queen of the class. In the end, the low price point and ability to engage students of every level makes Quiddler a wonderful literacy resource for the school library.

---

7 Ate 9

Published by: Out of the Box
Designed by: Maureen Hiron
Curricular area: Math
Year published: 2009
Number of players: 2–4
Playing time: 5–10 minutes

Used with permission from Out of the Box Publishing, Inc.

Sometimes the energy that a game creates makes it a wonderful fit with students. When the authenticity and joy of an experience brings students back during study halls and lunch, then you have a winning learning resource. Maureen Hiron's 7 Ate 9 taps into the frenetic energy of popular card games like slapjack and spit, pairing it with an almost instinctual application of addition and subtraction within a defined number set.

In the game, students are trying to rid their hand of cards as fast as they can by playing them onto a community pile in the center of the table. Each card features two key pieces of information: the card's main value, which is between one and ten, and a modifying value featured in the corners. Because ten is the highest number, students may have to wrap around the beginning or end of the set to find both possible values. As an example, a card may have a value of eight with a ± three modifier. If this is the current face-up card in the community pile, then the next playable card would be either a five or a one (eleven). Players start the game with an empty hand, simultaneously drawing from their own personal draw pile as they try to play cards onto the pile. It is through keen observation and a swift mathematical processing that students are able to quickly play through their hand of cards.

The fast pace of 7 Ate 9 speaks to the game's accessibility and utility. From start to finish, students can easily learn and play the game in less than ten minutes. Within this flurry of a fun and fluid information environment, students are developing a mastery of mathematical applications. Teachers will love this game's curricular strengths as students have to engage with and apply math to problems rapidly within a closed set, while students will revel in the frenetic race as they refine their math skills so they can get cards down more quickly each time they play—7 Ate 9 is a win-win situation all around.

The Suitcase Detectives (Kofferdetektive)

Published by: HABA—Habermaaß GmbH
Designed by: Guido Hoffmann
Curricular area: Science
Year published: 2008
Number of players: 2–4
Playing time: 15 minutes

Used with permission from HABA—Habermaaß GmbH

Student participation in activities that promote investigative inquiry through observation and deduction is an important stepping-stone for their growth as scientific thinkers. Wrapping that experience in a suitcase just makes it that much more fun. Guido Hoffmann's Suitcase Detectives is a unique game of observation and deduction that has students try to determine which objects Percy Pilferer, the notorious pickpocket, has stolen from a suitcase.

To play, students first select eight objects to be used for the round. These objects are similar to what you might see in shadow portraits. Because this is a game for younger students, each object is unique and very recognizable. Once the objects have been decided on, they are stashed away in the suitcase, which, cleverly enough, is the game box itself. Each student prepares their deck of cards, which features pictures of all the objects in the game, by removing any of the objects not being used this round. Now we start detecting!

Each round, one player takes on the role of Percy and secretly removes two objects from the suitcase. It is up to the rest of the players to determine which objects were stolen by examining what was left behind. Inside the suitcase is a blue opaque sheet that covers the secret compartment, making it difficult to see the remaining objects clearly. Additionally, the suitcase is small, so many of the objects are overlapping. The resulting view is a rather large, dark mass with various recognizable pieces protruding. Students work within a time frame, using their skills of observation and deduction to discover the missing objects, scoring a point for each correct answer.

The Suitcase Detectives is a refreshing approach to some fundamental scientific skills. It makes these concepts easily accessible to students of a very young age while keeping them fun and enjoyable. With the aid of a document camera, this can make a wonderful learning activity for a whole class of students, as volunteers share how they worked their way to the correct answer. For play purposes, this is a game that makes a great science center for a small group of students. The center can even include "detective pads" for students to record their observations to share with the other students.

10 Days in . . .
Published by: Out of the Box
Designed by: Aaron Weissblum and Alan R. Moon
Curricular area: Geography
Year published: 2003
Number of players: 2–4
Playing time: 30 minutes

Used with permission from Out of the Box Publishing, Inc.

10 Days in . . . is a series of games that includes 10 Days in Africa, 10 Days in Asia, 10 Days in Europe, and 10 Days in the USA. In each game, players are trying to make connections between different areas of the map using destination and travel tiles so that, when finished, the tiles are arranged to form a complete ten-day journey through that geographic locale.

Game play is exceedingly simple, with each player swapping a tile out of their lineup with either one of three face-up tiles or with the draw pile. Each player's goal is to have a travel itinerary of valid connections between locales. To make connections, players can walk between neighboring areas, fly between similarly colored destinations with a matching colored airplane, use a ship tile to sail on a particular body of water, or use a train tile to travel between countries on a rail line.

The 10 Days series is a great small-group game that will engage elementary students and appease any critical administrative eyes. Soon, students will be flexing their geography muscles as they scour countries and continents looking for ways to make their destinations connect. In addition to tapping into prior knowledge, players are also learning to adapt and reassess their approach based on currently available country tiles. It is this flexible application of geography that makes the 10 Days series a must-have for any elementary school library game collection.

Top Recommended Games for Middle School

Grades 6–8

Amun-Re

Published by: Rio Grande Games and Hans im Glück
Designed by: Reiner Knizia
Curricular area: World history
Year published: 2003
Number of players: 3–5
Playing time: 90 minutes

Games can excel at capturing the flavor of ancient civilizations and breathing life into them. While they may not always offer a fully faithful rendition, they do provide an interactive context for what students are learning in the classroom. Reiner Knizia's Amun-Re brings the age of pharaohs and pyramids to the table with critical choices and a good deal of strategy.

In Amun-Re, students play as pharaohs trying to build their legacy and influence throughout the Old and New Kingdoms. Each round, players bid for parcels of land bordering the Nile. They use this land to sow crops, harvest goods, and build pyramids honoring their rule. Each tract of land differs, depending on its relationship to the Nile; those bordering the river tend to be more fertile and provide a greater potential for farming, while those farther away rely more on trade for their income.

After purchasing land, players have a chance to develop by adding farmers, which translates into more income during the harvest, and building pyramids, which gives victory points at the end of the game. Lastly, a monetary offering is made to the temple, which influences the harvest and income earned from farmers and caravans.

The first three rounds mark the Old Kingdom. Players score at the end of the third round, and the New Kingdom begins with only the pyramids standing the test of time. Students play an additional three rounds, rebuilding upon the lands of their forefathers and score one final time.

Amun-Re creates both a challenging experience for middle school students and the educators introducing it. While the game does require an initial investment of time to teach the mechanics and rules, it is well within the abilities of the middle school students whose curriculum it targets. Together with other games, Amun-Re can create a wonderful collection supporting an ancient civilizations unit. In addition, the game uses language-independent pieces, which make this a great choice for using with English language learners as well.

---

duck! duck! GO!

Published by: APE Games
Designed by: Kevin G. Nunn
Curricular areas: Math and technology
Year published: 2008
Number of players: 2–6
Playing time: 30 minutes

Used with permission from APE Games

Sometimes the best way to get your head around something is to come at it from a completely different approach, to strip away the layers until you get to the essence of the experience. A student's initial foray into twenty-first-century skills such as logic, sequencing, and programming can be intimidating, so finding ways to make these concepts more accessible can help students struggling with these concepts. Enter stage left, one swarthy pirate duck.

In Kevin Nunn's duck! duck! GO!, players are racing a custom rubber duck around the bathtub, attempting to touch all of the buoys before finishing on the drain. The bathtub is a modular board, made up of several double-sided pieces that can be put together in a number of different configurations, making for a good amount of replayability.

Each turn, all of the students secretly select one of the three cards in their hand to program their duck's movements and then play them simultaneously. The cards feature the starting position, direction, and movement path for their ducks, along with a priority number. Starting with the lowest priority number, students take turns moving their ducks according to the paths on their cards. If the ducks hit a wall or another duck they stop, spin one hundred and eighty degrees, and end their turn. The advanced game introduces a bird dog, which provides some tactical opportunities for the player farthest behind in the race.

One possible modification for a whole-class activity is to combine several copies of the game together, forming one large board with multiple buoys and drains. Students would start on, but not be confined to, a section of the board and work toward touching an agreed-upon number of buoys before racing toward the nearest drain for a victory. Another alternative with a single copy is a relay race with students split into several teams and switching control when each buoy is touched. Here students are making group decisions, building their choices of the combined strengths of the team.

The game's flexibility helps facilitate implementation in the classroom, while the light and whimsical theme provides an easy entry point for students to some fundamental mathematics and technology skills. Because of this, students are able to interact with more complex directional and spatial problems and practice sequential movement programming within a dynamic learning environment.

LetterFlip
Published by: Out of the Box
Designed by: Ruddell Designs
Curricular area: ELA
Year published: 2004
Number of players: 2
Playing time: 30 minutes

Used with permission from Out of the Box Publishing, Inc.

Sometimes a variation on something simple can open the doors to learning. Part hangman, part Guess Who, and all word skill, LetterFlip is a classically inspired exercise in deduction and decoding.

In this two-player game, each student has a list of progressively longer words that the opposing player is trying to guess one letter at a time. To help them, players have a plastic tray with the letters of the alphabet they use to flip down for wrong guesses. No *h*? Flip it down! Right guesses stay up and wield their guesser additional information, such as frequency. Each letter has a tab that slides up to reveal stars. When a letter is correctly guessed, the player also reveals how often the letter appears in the word. In addition to guessing unknown letters, a student can also ask a letter's position in the word.

These seemingly small pieces come together in all the right ways, pushing students to draw on their word-building and decoding skills. If a student is working on a four-letter word with two *o*'s and a *k*, she can start to formulate what probable letter arrangements can be made from the letters. The two *o*'s are most likely in the middle with the *k* falling at the end. This lack of information, unlike hangman and other games where the visual clues are there, prompts a more demanding engagement with word structure and families.

While not revolutionary in its concept, LetterFlip is executed exceedingly well. The game is not only fun, it can be a valuable vocabulary tool.

While the publishers provide an ample number of cards at two difficulty levels, the player trays can easily be used to review vocabulary terms for any content area. Whether playing head-to-head or working in teams, using the stock lists or custom ones, students are sure to get a lexical workout.

Nanofictionary

Published by: Looney Labs
Designed by: Andrew Looney
Curricular area: ELA
Year published: 2002
Number of players: 3–6
Playing time: 30 minutes

Used with permission from Looney Labs

Games in the storytelling genre often provide a flexible framework for engaging students with story elements and the creative writing process. One example is Andrew Looney's Nanofictionary, a card game in which students develop little stories from various plot elements encountered through play. Traditionally, writing exercises provide a prompt for student response, or if no prompt is provided, students have the luxury to create drafts and rewrites as they develop their story. In Nanofictionary, students must actively develop, rearrange, rethink, and rewrite their story within the confines of the game. The experience is similar to improvisational exercises where participants must construct a story from random plot device cards. In Nanofictionary, these cards form the building blocks that, along with a mortar mix of creativity and imagination, combine to create each student's story.

To start, players are dealt a hand of cards in preparation for the writing phase in which they must construct a story using the game's four plot devices (character, setting, problem, and resolution). During this phase, players will be drawing, playing, and discarding cards as they attempt to combine elements that make for an interesting tale. New story elements can shift the focus of the students, prompting them to refine or reimagine their tale midphase. Additionally, as stories are developed by the other players, they can serve as a catalyst for students to refine their tales.

Once all of the students have finished, it is time to spin some yarns. Each student tells a little story incorporating the cards they played. Not using all of the cards is all right, as long as each of the four plot devices is included. After every student has told his tale, the awards phase takes place, with students giving out awards to each of the other players. (Students can't award their own stories.) Other students who were listening but not playing can stand in as jurors and award points as well.

Students combine all their points earned, along with any bonus for finishing quickly, and determine the winner.

Nanofictionary provides a fluid environment within which students can put into practice many of the fundamental ELA skills they are developing in the classroom. The game's mechanics are reflective of the flexible information environments that are becoming more prevalent in today's world. By using games such as Nanofictionary, educators have access to tools that can marry their curriculum with meaningful examples of these contemporary environments.

Numbers League
Published by: Bent Castle Workshops
Designed by: Chris Pallace and Ben Crenshaw
Curricular area: Math
Year published: 2007
Number of players: 2–4
Playing time: 30 minutes

Used with permission from Bent Castle Workshops

Numbers League is a superhero-themed card game that gives elementary and middle school students a platform for fine-tuning fundamental math skills through play. In the game, students literally put together superheroes in an effort to capture a host of villains loose in Infinity City. With the clever manipulation of numbers and some heroic accessories, students will soon be learning to master math.

In the game, superheroes are constructed from the various head, body, and leg parts from within the deck. Part of the appeal of the game is mixing and matching to build interesting and fun combinations. Each body part has an individual value, with the superhero's total value being the combination of all three. As students build their team, they have the opportunity to capture villains by combining the values of all or some of their heroes, which is not always as easy as it sounds. Luckily students have an arsenal of accessories available to use as onetime modifiers on their heroes.

As the game progresses, the challenge becomes finding the right combinations of heroes and deciding which heroes to play modifiers on in order to reach the different villains. As an example, one villain could have a value of twenty-seven. A student may have built three superheroes with values of four, five, and two. Together these are shy of the villain's twenty-seven value, but the student has a pair of boots that provide a onetime x5 multiplier. Looking at the different possibilities, the student decides to play the boots on the hero valued at four, raising its value to twenty and allowing, with the addition of the other heroes, the villain's capture.

Mathematics requires a certain amount of repetition for success. Numbers League moves beyond success toward mastery, as students develop a mathematical flexibility that is representative of math's use in the real world. The game's strong curricular connections, low price point, and reasonable playing time make it easy to include as a full-class activity.

Oregon

Published by: Rio Grande Games and Hans im Glück
Designed by: Henrik Berg and Ase Berg
Curricular area: Math
Year published: 2007
Number of players: 2–4
Playing time: 45 minutes

Cover scan courtesy of Carl Anderson

Sometimes first impressions can be misleading. On the surface, Oregon presents itself as a game with a light theme about the exploration and development of the West during the mid-1800s. While the theme is notable, it is the clever modification of the Cartesian coordinate system that warrants this game's place on the list.

In Oregon, students settle and develop the untapped expanse of the Oregon territory. The game board, a colorful map composed of various geographical features, is overlaid with a grid of columns and rows creating rectangular intersections. Each column features a symbol, and these are repeated in a different pattern for the rows. The combination of these symbols creates the coordinates for students to place buildings and farmers.

Farmers are placed by playing two cards with symbols. Because the symbols are repeated on both the x and the y axes, the farmer can be played in either of the two corresponding intersections. For example, a student could play a farmer in the fire/eagle section or the eagle/fire section. Buildings require only one symbol card and a building card. They can be played anywhere along the row or column that matches the symbol as long as it matches the corresponding terrain type: mines on mountains, docks on water, and so on. Farmers score points for the player who places them, but buildings score points for any player whose farmer is adjacent to a building when it is placed.

While having a slight disconnect between the theme and mechanics, the game is well worth the investment due to the unique use of an often underserved mathematical skill. While the game can be played in teams, the real value comes from students developing play strategies as the game progresses. Which set of coordinates is most beneficial is continually in flux as play moves around the table, requiring students to actively use math throughout the course of the game.

Shadows over Camelot

Published by: Days of Wonder
Designed by: Serge Laget and Bruno Cathala
Curricular area: ELA
Year published: 2005
Number of players: 3–7
Playing time: 90 minutes

© Days of Wonder, Inc.

Together a noble band of brave knights strives to fend off the onslaught of forces besieging Camelot while keeping ever-watchful eyes on their own brethren. There are whispers of a traitor in their midst. One of their own is striving to offset the company's efforts to fill the halls of Camelot with the glories of triumph.

So the stage is set for Serge Laget and Bruno Cathala's cooperative adventure. Each player is one of the knights of Camelot who, along with his peers, is seeking to stem back bad fortune, treachery, assault, invasion, and dishonor. Failure is ensured if the players do not work together and take advantage of their unique qualities.

Game play is advanced through a variety of quests that the knights can take, earning them white swords (which advance the group toward victory), cards (which are the heart of the game play), and the coveted relics (Holy Grail, Lancelot's Armor, and Excalibur). A key twist to the game is the potential of a traitor working to undermine and sabotage all efforts of the loyal knights of Camelot.

Each turn, players must choose a bad and good action to perform. The bad actions add to the ever-increasing obstacles holding the knight back from victory, while the good actions are never enough on their own to put the knights over the top. It is only through coordination, communication, and teamwork that the students have any hope of turning the tide toward victory.

Shadows over Camelot succeeds at challenging students to engage with each other, using oral language for persuasive, informational, argumentative, and critical communication. These are valuable skills to develop for academic success and are needed even more during the middle school years when students are often self-conscious and unsure of themselves. While this game can be played over the course of two days, the experience becomes diluted on the second day as students have to try to restoke the fires of tension and camaraderie. It works best if students are able to play straight through a game, perhaps in an after-school club or during a double period. Initially, this is a game that the librarian or teacher needs to learn and teach to the students, but after the students learn the game they will be eager to replay and share the experience with their peers.

Ticket to Ride

Published by: Days of Wonder
Designed by: Alan R. Moon
Curricular area: Geography
Year published: 2004
Number of players: 2–5
Playing time: 45 minutes

© Days of Wonder, Inc.

Considered one of the quintessential gateway games, Ticket to Ride is a model of sophisticated simplicity. Part of the "train game" genre, the game strikes a fine balance between accessibility and curricular content. In comparison to the 10 Days series featured on the elementary list, Ticket to Ride tips the scales more toward fun, whereas 10 Days weighs in more on content.

In the game, students work to connect cities listed on several route cards they hold in their hands. Each player's route cards are secret, so none of the players knows where the others are working toward unless someone makes it apparent through their actions. Cities are connected by playing the correct number and color of train cards shown on the board, with longer routes claimed through a contiguous string of connections between the necessary cities. As more connections are made, the more challenging it becomes to complete the full runs of uninterrupted connections needed to claim a route. Players need to employ an agile approach to problem solving as they work through their options, often finding alternative avenues to their goal.

One of the strengths of the game is its accessibility. With only three possible actions to choose from, introducing and getting students involved in the game is quick and simple. Because of this simplicity, the game moves briskly as students have fun applying basic geography within a challenging game environment. Multiple copies make for a great geography review activity for the whole class, while a single copy can provide an enjoyable enrichment activity for students struggling with the content.

Tribune: Primus Inter Pares
Published by: Fantasy Flight Games
Designed by: Karl-Heinz Schmiel
Curricular area: World history
Year published: 2007
Number of players: 2–5
Playing time: 60 minutes

Used with permission from Fantasy Flight Games

The ancient Roman Empire was a stew pot of factions, each with its own beliefs and agendas but unified under Roman citizenship. Gaining support and favor from these factions was a sure path toward power and one way to acquire the title of tribune. Karl-Heinz Schmiel's game captures important aspects of the social and political landscape of ancient Rome for students as they maneuver and manipulate the various factions on their ascension from patrician to tribune.

In Tribune, students are members of patrician families struggling for political power, eager to gain the title of tribune. This status is achieved by gaining the support of the different factions throughout the game. While it is not necessary to hold each faction's support for the course of the game, the timing of when they are gained can be important, as holding several factions simultaneously grants valuable resources and marks of distinction.

It is through this ebb and flow of faction support that students begin to satisfy the victory conditions for the game. At the beginning of each game, students will select a card that outlines the different objectives available for reaching victory. Each card will indicate how many individual objectives are needed to win the game. So while there may be seven objectives, students will only need to obtain a certain number of them, depending on the number of players in the game. It then becomes their choice which objectives they pursue on their quest for power.

Game play is a mixture of worker placement and set collection, as students take turns placing their followers on different areas of the city to gather faction support cards. The board features a mixture of open and hidden information that students need to evaluate and utilize as part of their decision-making process. As students collect cards, they can use them to gain control of factions by laying down either a higher sum value or a greater number of cards than the player who currently controls the faction.

Tribune, like many other historical games, is not a fully accurate representation, but it does capture some elements for reinforcement. Tribune's use of language and social strata is a valuable addition to units studying ancient Rome, because it provides students an opportunity to interact with elements of the curriculum not always found in other activities. The game can be incorporated as a part of a unit covering ancient Rome or it can be combined with other ancient civilization games as a collective set of resources. If using Tribune alone, students can play alone or in pairs. If used as part of a set of ancient civilization games, then students can cycle between games each day for an effective review of many elements from the course.

VisualEyes

Published by: Buffalo Games, Inc.
Designed by: Keith Dugald and
                Steve Pickering
Curricular area: ELA
Year published: 2003
Number of players: 2–8
Playing time: 30 minutes

Used with permission from Buffalo Games, Inc.

Differentiated instruction is an important part of today's educational landscape. As educators strive to meet the learning needs of all the students in their class, unique approaches to curricular content are valued for their instructional potential. Keith Dugald and Steve Pickering's VisualEyes offers a different approach to thinking about language through the creative combination of images to form words and phrases.

The game centers around a set of extra-large dice that feature a variety of pictures on their faces. The goal of the game is to combine images from pairs of dice to create familiar words or phrases. Each round a player covers the game box and rolls all of the dice to get the game started. One die lets students know what mode of play the current round will be. If the mode die says fast play, then students must plan to make words or phrases from pairs of dice as quickly as they can. When a student is successful, they call out their answer and take the pair of corresponding dice. When no one is able to make any more new words or phrases, each player scores a point for every pair of dice they have. Slow play is similar to Scattergories, with students writing down as many words or phrases they can make from the dice in the box before the timer runs out. When time is up, players score points for any unique acceptable answers they have on their sheet.

Simple and fast, VisualEyes allows students to create and interact with language in a very different way than they are accustomed. Each picture is open for interpretation, allowing students to be creative in the way they approach language creation. A snowflake and jacket could be *winter coat,* while a snowflake and a heart could be *coldhearted.* Students can begin to see how perception and interpretation play a role in language, and it is this semantic flexibility that makes VisualEyes a wonderful educational tool.

Top Recommended Games for High School

Grades 9–12

Antike

Published by: Rio Grande Games and Eggertspiele
Designed by: Mac Gerdts
Curricular area: Global studies
Year published: 2005
Number of players: 2–6
Playing time: 120 minutes

© Rio Grande Games

Ancient Greece and Rome are empires of legend. Their political and military machines spread outward, claiming new lands, resources, and people. To be successful, their leaders had to find a balance between expansion and the defense of their lands. Equally important was an internal growth of science and culture, which provided the motivation and technology to both support and sustain the empire. Mac Gerdts's Antike creates a playable snapshot of these situations, allowing students to explore the push and pull of expanding an empire and sustaining its growth.

The game features two playable areas of development: the Roman Empire and the empire of Alexander the Great. Students play one of the nations involved in these theaters of power, including the Phoenicians, Persians, Greeks, Babylonians, Romans, and others. The goal of each is to grow its empire through expansion and internal development, gaining notable figures from history as it reaches certain achievements through the development of knowledge, territories gained, cities toppled, and internal growth.

The game utilizes a unique mechanic called a *rondel* that creates a perfect information game by showing each player's potential choices for the turn. The rondel is a segmented circle with an action featured in each of the segments. On each turn, players can select an action that falls within three spaces clockwise from their current position. Actions beyond the three spaces are available at a cost of one gold piece for each additional space. This mechanism allows players to plan ahead for future moves while taking into consideration the potential moves of their opponents.

Despite its visual similarity to Risk, Antike plays more like traditional strategy games such as chess or go. Students are interacting with information in a logical and strategic way, while drawing from their knowledge of ancient civilizations to help guide their decisions. The game does lend itself to teams, but this can slow down playing time for a full game. One possible variation is to set the game up to reflect situations from the class curriculum, allowing students to an opportunity to experience, in a small way, the nature of an empire.

Battlestar Galactica
Published by: Fantasy Flight Games
Designed by: Corey Konieczka
Curricular area: ELA
Year published: 2008
Number of players: 3–6
Playing time: 120 minutes

Used with permission from Fantasy Flight Games

Popular culture will always have appeal, but when popular culture is recycled it is usually because there is some quality behind the experience. Corey Konieczka's Battlestar Galactica is a cooperative game based around the reimplemented television show of the same name. Most often, licensed games are a quick way to tap into what is often a waning interest, but occasionally one is done well and will stand on its own merits. Battlestar Galactica is an example of the latter, skillfully leveraging the show's rich story line while not requiring familiarity to enjoy game play.

The backstory for the game is that the majority of the human race has been eradicated by sentient machines (Cylons) that were created by man. A small remnant of humanity is on the run, seeking a new home on Earth as the Cylons relentlessly pursue them. Unfortunately for the humans, they are short on time, resources, and luck. Additionally, they have recently discovered that the Cylons have developed the ability to create machines that accurately resemble humans, leaving no one worthy of trust despite their desperate need to rely on each other.

Each player takes on the role of one of the characters from the story, each of whom has a detailed background and brings unique abilities and weaknesses to the game. They also receive a loyalty card that lets them know if they are a human, a Cylon, or a Cylon sympathizer. The difference between this game and other cooperative games such as Shadows over Camelot is that in Battlestar there will be a Cylon or perhaps even two, as players receive additional loyalty cards midway through the game.

As the game progresses, human players must coordinate their abilities and resources to effectively deal with a variety of events and crises they encounter, including Cylon attacks, sabotage, food and water shortages, and civil unrest. Each turn, they hope to manage these problems as they try to make their way toward finding Earth, all the while avoiding the Cylon players' attempts at stopping them.

It is the quality of experience created by a mixture of mechanics and theme that makes this a jewel of a game. The certainty of a traitor combined with a well-executed buildup of pressure creates a thick level of tension as students struggle to work together while never fully trusting each other. From the very beginning, students must critically evaluate each piece of information and action they encounter to help them make decisions in an environment where every decision matters. Character development is also critical during the game, as students develop an understanding of motivations and loyalties through cooperation and posturing. In the end, Battlestar Galactica combines the story elements of a great novel, the scintillation of a movie, and the interaction of the theater to provide a rich and vibrant growth experience for students.

Bolide

Published by: Rio Grande Games and
                   Ghenos Games
Designed by: Alfredo Genovese
Curricular areas: Science and math
Year published: 2005
Number of players: 2–8
Playing time: 120 minutes

Used with permission from Ghenos Games

Racing games often combine tactical decisions with a heavy dose of luck, but Bolide refines the genre down to pure strategy by basing its movement mechanics around the science of the sport. In the game, up to eight players can compete on one of two racetracks, applying logic, physics, and mathematics as they make their way toward the finish line.

Bolide comes with a large double-sided board featuring racetracks on either side. Each track is overlaid with a grid whose intersections provide the movement points for the game. Students control a race car and a marker that reflects their momentum and movement potential. Each movement made with their car is first in relation to and then mirrored by their momentum marker.

After the initial move, each further movement along the track must finish within a two-point radius around the marker. If the car moves past the marker, the student is accelerating, and if the car finishes behind the marker, he is slowing down. Once the student moves his car, he then mirrors the exact movements made with his car using his momentum marker, starting from where the car just finished. So, if a student moved three spaces over and four spaces up, his marker would mirror that movement from where the car finished, providing a new range of possible moves.

While the movement mechanism is based on science, the explanation does not need to be mired in the language. The rules are simple enough that they can be explained without a physics teacher, but the curricular connections are strong enough that that teacher will not want to be left out. When implementing, multiple copies are the key, as the suggested two-hour time does not apply with the full complement of eight players. The more players involved, the more time is required to plan and execute movements, so more games with fewer players is better for the classroom.

1960: The Making of the President

Published by: Z-Man Games, Inc.
Designed by: Christian Leonhard and
                Jason Matthews
Curricular areas: Global studies and
                participation in
                government
Year published: 2007
Number of players: 2
Playing time: 180 minutes

Used with permission from Z-Man Games, Inc.

In 1960: The Making of the President, students have an opportunity to re-create one of the most memorable elections of the last century. This was a delicate time in U.S. history when the country was in the middle of the Cold War and struggling with issues of civil rights, foreign policy, and the economy. It is in the midst of this fragile climate that students take on the role of one of the two candidates vying for election, Richard Nixon or John F. Kennedy.

The game features an electoral map of the United States, with the vote counts reflecting their standings as of 1960. This map serves as the battleground for the game, as each candidate works to build state support into and after the debates, hoping to carry enough states through to win the election. On the road to the White House, the candidates will need to campaign diligently while also investing resources in advertising and building support on the issues.

Moving all of this along is a deck of cards featuring primary source images and events timely to the election. These cards can be used to either trigger the featured event or to invest in various actions. How students choose to use the cards, based on their effects and the party they favor, is a large part of player strategy.

Being a two-player game, 1960 requires some slight modifications to transition to a larger group experience. Instead of one student playing as the candidate, a small group can play as campaign managers working together to advance their candidate toward the presidency. This helps students manage the different aspects of the game by splitting them among the team. Additionally, because this game will play out over the course of several days, students can use an outline map of the United States to track each candidate's support in the states between plays.

1960 is a sophisticated game that requires a heavy commitment of time to set up, teach, and play through. That being said, there are very few experiences that provide the level of depth and engagement that it provides. After taking part in the game experience, students come away with an understanding of U.S. history and the electoral process that is hard to match.

Once upon a Time
Published by: Atlas Games
Designed by: Andrew Rilstone, James Wallis, and
Richard Lambert
Curricular area: ELA
Year published: 1993
Number of players: 2–6
Playing time: 30 minutes

Once upon a Time is a trademark of John Nephew, used by Trident, Inc. d/b/a Atlas Games under license, and used here with permission

Fairy tales have been an important part of human culture for centuries. They not only provide opportunities for exposure to new ideas and language, but they also capture the imagination with their fanciful narratives and dark undertones. Once upon a Time is an ever-changing storytelling game set in this fairy-tale world, where students attempt to weave a tale toward their secret "Happy Ever After."

Each player is dealt a hand of storytelling cards that feature different elements commonly used in fairy tales and one "Happy Ever After" card, which is the ending to their story. All of the storytelling elements are grouped into five different categories: characters, items, places, aspects, and events. To begin, one student starts the tale, trying to guide the story toward her ending by using the different storytelling cards in her hand.

As the student is telling her story, she can play cards from her hand that she is able to incorporate. If she successfully uses all of her cards and finishes the story using her ending, she is able to go out and win the game.

While this sounds simple enough, this is not a solitaire game and other players are a part of the game as well.

Each of the other players has the ability to interrupt the story if at any point it mentions an element from one of their storytelling cards. They may also have special interrupt cards that can be used when it matches a particular group that was played. When interrupted, the current storyteller must draw a card while the new storyteller continues the story toward his ending.

With each draw, students must find ways to incorporate new information into the elements in their hand. Additionally, students remain engaged when it is not their turn, as they actively listen for ways to intervene and consider the possibilities for interweaving their storytelling elements with the story at hand.

Once upon a Time makes storytelling a fun and interactive experience. The game can easily scale up to handle larger groups or be used with several smaller groups as warm-up activities. Because the game consists of story elements, there are a host of modifications for incorporating it into different learning environments. The game can be played cooperatively, removing the competitive element, with students adding their storytelling elements to the group's story. Students can also add their own elements to the game through an expansion, pushing the creativity envelope even further.

Pandemic

Published by: Z-Man Games, Inc.
Designed by: Matt Leacock
Curricular areas: Science and geography
Year published: 2008
Number of players: 2–4
Playing time: 45 minutes

Used with permission from Z-Man Games, Inc.

The second cooperative game on the high school list, Matt Leacock's Pandemic, marries infectious diseases and global geography in a fast and frenzied race to save the world. Students are specialists working for the Centers for Disease Control and Prevention out of Atlanta, Georgia. Four virulent diseases have broken out all over the world, and it is up to them to find the cures before the situation goes too far. The game is played on a map of the world, with a number of high-population cities on each continent sharing connections. These connections are avenues for the four diseases to spread throughout the course of the game.

The four diseases, represented by different colored cubes, are placed in cities as the result of cards drawn from an infection deck. Each city can only hold three of any one type of disease; when a fourth disease cube needs to be added, an outbreak occurs and instead a cube from that disease is added to any connected city. Of course, if there are already three cubes of that color in a neighboring city, another outbreak occurs. The potential for disaster is always imminent.

As with players in Shadows over Camelot, each student will be advancing both the positive and negative components of the game on their turn. The mechanics of the game make it easy for the diseases to spread quickly and trigger outbreaks. Students will need to really think about and discuss their limited actions to maximize their effect. Each player can take up to four actions during his turn to travel, build research stations, treat infected areas, or find a cure. The players are victorious if they are able to cure all four diseases before a certain number of outbreaks occur.

Pandemic illuminates the delicate barriers that keep worldwide outbreaks at bay. It pushes students to reflect on the pros and cons of living in a global community; ease of travel helps facilitate the spread of disease but it also aids in arresting its growth as well. Because of the reasonable playing time, multiple copies of the game can easily provide a whole-class experience within a period, but the game can also be played with a small group or solo as well.

Portrayal

Published by: Braincog, Inc.
Designed by: Amanda Kohout and William Jacobson
Curricular area: ELA
Year published: 2006
Number of players: 3–10
Playing time: 45 minutes

Used with permission from Braincog, Inc.

Amanda Kohout and William Jacobson's game mixes comprehension with comic styling and brings it to the classroom. This is a description and drawing game that rewards listening skills above artistic ones, as players strive to be as detail-oriented as they can to score points.

Students take turns describing as accurately as they can an outrageously elaborate picture to the rest of the players within ninety seconds. For each picture, there are a set of ten details that are kept secret from both the student describing (the Portrayer) and the students drawing (the Artists). These details will be the judging criteria when time has elapsed. The pictures are detailed enough that there is never enough time to describe each element, requiring quick judgments to be made on what elements seem important. When time is up, players exchange drawings, and the Portrayer reveals the details for scoring. Each detail included in the drawing scores a point for the artist, and if at least one artist included the detail, the Portrayer also scores a point.

Portrayal is a fast and fun game that strengthens a student's descriptive language and critical listening skills. It can easily scale up to handle a whole class of students and makes a wonderful warm-up exercise before tests or activities that require an attentive ear. Because the game comes with so many image cards, it has a very high replay value, making Portrayal a game that will engage students in the classroom and library for many years.

Power Grid

Published by: Rio Grande Games and 2F Spiele
Designed by: Friedemann Friese
Curricular areas: Science and economics
Year published: 2004
Number of players: 2–6
Playing time: 120 minutes

© Rio Grande Games

Friedemann Friese's Power Grid brings to the table the elegant interplay of economics and energy, illuminating for students the sometimes harsh realities of resource management. In the game, players develop power companies by building up the capacity and resources needed to provide service to cities within their network. The more cities students are able to power, the more capital they can make. Of course, they will need capital in order to expand their network and acquire the resources needed to power it.

To begin play, students first bid on power plants that use different resource types, including fossil fuels, nuclear, garbage, and wind. The availability of plants is dependent on which map is being used. After purchasing a plant, students then need to buy resources from the market to power their plants. Initially, coal and oil are readily available and very inexpensive, making those types of plants a wise investment early in the game. As players purchase resources, their prices go up due to demand placed on the market. This can affect a student's ability to power cities with less efficient plants that require a high number of expensive resources.

Lastly, students spend money to incorporate more cities into their network by paying costs to build into cities and any additional costs needed to connect. When each student has had a chance to expand her network, then students can use their resources to power cities for profit. At the end of each turn, the market's resources get replenished depending on how far into the game players have progressed. Play continues until a certain number of cities have been connected, with the winner being the player who can power the most cities.

Power Grid presents students with a sophisticated model of a market economy and some strong conversational points surrounding environmental science as well. This is another game that requires a larger investment on the part of librarians and teachers, with the gaming experience extending across two or three class periods. As with any of the longer game resources, investing a day to have the students learn the mechanics of the game by playing a round is worthwhile. Students then can focus on playing the game and engaging with the curriculum rather than struggling to learn and play at the same time.

Through the Ages

Published by: FRED Distribution
Designed by: Vlaada (Vladimír) Chvátil
Curricular area: Global studies
Year published: 2006
Number of players: 2–4
Playing time: 240 minutes

Used with permission from FRED Distribution

In the curriculum, the development and growth of human civilization is often encountered and digested in small, isolated pieces. It is then up to the educators and students to find a way to step back and find a more connected picture of who we are, where we have been, and where we are going. Chvátil's Through the Ages successfully takes on the daunting task of providing a platform for students to understand that progression by developing a civilization from antiquity to the modern age.

Students start out in antiquity under a despotic rule. They do not have a large population, their food and resource production is very limited, and they are militarily weak and culturally poor. How they choose to grow and develop over the course of the game is completely open—although there are some considerations to keep in mind.

As your population grows, it will need food to sustain itself and religion and entertainment to keep it content. Each age brings new and more efficient technologies that help meet these needs. In addition to food and happiness, students need to manage their resource production and investment in science. Resources are needed for producing buildings and arming military units, and knowledge accumulated through investment in science allows students to make advancements in their technologies.

Needless to say, this is a bear of a game that when taken on requires a large commitment of time for students to come to understand and successfully complete the game. That time can be condensed into a week or played out over the course of a semester, with students planning their moves between classes. The game instructions do a wonderful job of breaking the game into introductory, advanced, and full versions. The introductory version is easily playable over the course of a day or two and can provide students with the familiarity and comfort needed before progressing to the more sophisticated versions of the game. Through the Ages is a wonderful example of a game with a very high investment but whose return far outweighs its demands.

Ultimate Werewolf: Ultimate Edition

Published by: Bézier Games
Designed by: Ted Alspach
Curricular area: ELA
Year published: 2008
Number of players: 5–68
Playing time: 15–45 minutes

Used with permission from Bézier Games

Games are constructed story kits complete with theme, setting, and characters. While some games tell a story, Ultimate Werewolf gives students the opportunity to act one out. The game sets the stage for a rich character experience filled with role-playing, deduction, persuasion, and misdirection.

The premise of the game is that students are villagers in a small remote area in the countryside. Lately, people have been disappearing in the night as werewolves have infiltrated the village. Each morning, the village awakes to find another person missing and must select one member of the village to convict of lycanthropy and lynch.

The game itself consists of a set of role cards and rules. While there are several versions of the game available, we have included the Bézier Games edition because the abundance of role cards provides the capacity to handle up to three classes of students and the rule book is the best source for learning to run the game, hands down.

Game play is broken down into two phases each turn: night and day. The heart of the game centers around the daytime conversations as students accuse others and defend themselves. An important thing to note is that an effective game hinges on two things: a good moderator to guide the story and students playing in the spirit of the game.

While the game components are the most minimal of any on the lists, it is also the game in need of the most modifications to be successful in the classroom. The language of the game may need to be softened so that villagers are "taken away" and potential werewolves are "locked up." Additionally, a few of the extra roles can be excluded, depending on the social atmosphere of the school district. That being said, Ultimate Werewolf excels at immersing students in narrative by not only making them characters but providing a strong motivation to participate. Because the game experience elicits creativity, character identification, and persuasive dialogue from students, it is a perfect choice for classroom creative and persuasive writing activities.

Glossary of Designer Board Game Terminology

Area control. A type of game mechanic in which players work toward controlling the most area in a playing space. It is a mechanic often used as a criterion for end-game victory conditions or for earning rewards during play. The use of area control can be found across all styles and genres of games, from abstract games like go to more thematic games like Richard Ulrich and Wolfgang Kramer's El Grande. As a learning experience, area control games provide students with the opportunity to think critically and be adaptive in developing and implementing strategies.

Cooperative play. A mechanic for player interaction that rewards, and often requires, working together for there to be any chance at a successful game resolution. Many times, each player will have some unique characteristic he can contribute, making how and when each player helps part of the game's strategy. Cooperative games are especially effective at building team skills and helping students see value in different opinions and approaches.

Gateway game. A game that is often used to introduce those unfamiliar with designer games with the genre. They often play in under an hour and have very few rules, while offering a level of strategy and interaction beyond expectations. This results in an easily accessible and often surprising game play experience that piques new players' interests in other designer games. The most often cited examples are Klaus-Jürgen Wrede's Carcassonne, Klaus Teuber's Settlers of Catan, and Alan R. Moon's Ticket to Ride.

Imperfect information. An element of game design in which the other players' actions and other relevant details are not accessible or reliable. Most games fall into this category, where players do not have knowledge of all the information available within the game. This lack of information results in players having to make inferences and speculative choices when making decisions and developing strategies.

Language independence. A game design choice that makes the game's components free of any textual content. Instead, more universally understood images, pictures, or symbols are used to convey meaning and directions during play. By utilizing language-independent games, schools providing services to a population of English language learners can bridge the language barrier and provide complex and engaging learning experiences to all of the students they instruct.

Mechanic. A set of rules that govern how an aspect of the game is played. Simpler games may only use a single mechanic, while more sophisticated ones can incorporate a blend of multiple mechanics. In terms of game design, the proper matching of mechanics and theme can combine to create a truly immersive game play experience. When examining a game's connections to learning standards, mechanics often relate to math and science standards.

Perfect information. An element of game design in which everything relevant to the game experience is made openly available for all of the players. Centered around strategic choices and logic, this gaming genre is but a small subset of games that includes classic titles such as go and chess, along with more contemporary games such as Alvydas Jakeliunas and Günter Cornett's Hey! That's My Fish!

Push (or press) your luck. A game mechanic that allows the player to select or take actions until either she chooses to stop or she meets a trigger point for an established negative consequence. Built into this model is an ever-increasing level of risk with each additional action. Incorporating games that employ this mechanic is an excellent way to introduce students to the concepts of risk management and mathematical probability.

Resource management. A set of game mechanics in which the players control and manipulate, according to a set of rules, available resources within the game in order to affect play in some way. This style of game allows students to experience economic concepts such as supply and demand, market economy, free trade, and scarcity.

Role selection. A game mechanic in which players select one or more roles each turn based on the actions or resources provided. Order of choice plays a heavy part in strategy development, especially when selected roles allow every player access to their benefits. To offset the potential power of first choice, role selection games will either rotate the starting player each turn or include starting as part of a handicapped choice in the game. Because of the unique nature of the roles, during the selection process students need to expand their focus beyond simply advancing their needs and goals and take into account how their selection might affect the needs and goals of other players as well.

Scalability. The ability of a game to maintain the intended play experience as more or fewer players are added. Some games may require slight modifications to account for varying numbers of players. Often, these variants will allow a smaller or larger number of players to enjoy the game without compromising the elegance of the game's mechanics. When the experience becomes broken (i.e., the game's difficulty drastically changes or too many modifications are needed to make it work), the game's scalability level has been reached. Some games are not scalable and only work for the recommended number of players, while others can easily accommodate more than the number stated on the box.

Simultaneous action selection. A game mechanic that allows for each player to select or execute an action at the same time. This removes any potential for an advantage being gained by modifying a player's choice based on the actions selected by the other players. Each decision for action is based on the last group action as a whole and not as the result of player order. This play mechanic introduces a certain level of unpredictability, especially if some form of player interaction is the result.

Theme. The story elements that provide meaning and context for the mechanical actions of the game. Themed games can vary not only in weight but in subject matter as well. Abstract games, on the other hand, are devoid of theme and stand alone on their merits and the enjoyability of their mechanics. When examining a game's connections to learning standards, theme will often create connections with the social studies and English and language arts curricula.

Tile placement. A game mechanic in which players draw and lay down tiles to either advance the game or to establish a playing area within which other actions can be taken. Klaus-Jürgen Wrede's Carcassonne is a classic example of the latter. Tile placement games are a great way to help students develop spatial skills as they match or create patterns with the tiles.

Traitor. A game mechanic commonly found in cooperative games that introduces a secret role meant to sow distrust and uncertainty among players. The potential effect of the traitor is directly proportional to the game's difficulty level and need for cooperation. This effect is heightened when the inclusion of the role is not a complete certainty. Students participating in a game experience that utilizes the traitor mechanic draw from and strengthen persuasive and evaluative language skills as well as develop more sophisticated social skills.

Victory points. An inclusive scoring mechanic used in many designer games to track each player's progress over the course of the game. By assigning point values to different aspects of the game and indicating victory conditions, designers allow all of the players to stay involved until the end-game conditions are met. Games utilizing victory points are a wise choice from a classroom management perspective, as the whole group will finish the learning experience at the same time.

Worker placement. A game mechanic in which players have a set number of pawns to place each turn. The placement of a pawn, or worker, usually provides access to an action or resource necessary for the progression of the game. When well executed as a game mechanic, players should not have enough pawns available to allow access to every desired action each turn. This scarcity helps students reflect on their needs and goals, teaching them how to prioritize and focus on efficiency.

List of Games Discussed

Download this list from the Web: www.ala.org/editions/extras/mayer10092.

Agricola
Published by: Z-Man Games, Inc.
Designed by: Uwe Rosenberg
Year published: 2007
Number of players: 1–5
Grade levels: Middle and high
school

Amun-Re
Published by: Rio Grande Games
and Hans im Glück
Designed by: Reiner Knizia
Year published: 2003
Number of players: 3–5
Grade levels: Middle and high
school

Android
Published by: Fantasy Flight Games
Designed by: Daniel Clark and
Kevin Wilson
Year published: 2008
Number of players: 3–5
Grade level: High school

Antike
Published by: Rio Grande Games
and Eggertspiele
Designed by: Mac Gerdts
Year published: 2005

Number of players: 2–6
Grade levels: Middle and high
school

**Arthur Saves the Planet:
One Step at a Time**
Published by: FRED Distribution
Designed by: Mike Siggins
Year published: 2008
Number of players: 2–5
Grade levels: Elementary and
middle school

Backseat Drawing
Published by: Out of the Box
Designed by: Catherine Rondeau
and Peggy Brown
Year published: 2008
Number of players: 4–10
Grade levels: Middle and high
school

Bamboleo
Published by: Rio Grande Games
and Zoch Verlag
Designed by: Jacques Zeimet
Year published: 1996
Number of players: 2–7
Grade levels: Middle and high
school

Battlestar Galactica
Published by: Fantasy Flight
Games
Designed by: Corey Konieczka
Year published: 2008
Number of players: 3–6
Grade level: High school

Bausack
Published by: Zoch Verlag
Designed by: Klaus Zoch
Year published: 1987
Number of players: 1–10
Grade levels: Middle and high
school

Bolide
Published by: Rio Grande Games
and Ghenos Games
Designed by: Alfredo Genovese
Year published: 2005
Number of players: 2–8
Grade level: High school

Brass
Published by: Warfrog Games and
FRED Distribution
Designed by: Martin Wallace
Year published: 2007
Number of players: 3–4
Grade level: High school

Carcassonne
Published by: Rio Grande Games
and Hans im Glück
Designed by: Klaus-Jürgen Wrede
Year published: 2000
Number of players: 2–5
Grade levels: Middle and high
school

Chicago Express
Published by: Rio Grande Games
and Queen Games
Designed by: Harry Wu

Year published: 2007
Number of players: 2–6
Grade levels: Middle and high
school

Colosseum
Published by: Days of Wonder
Designed by: Markus Lübke and
Wolfgang Kramer
Year published: 2007
Number of players: 3–5
Grade levels: Middle and high
school

Diplomacy
Published by: Avalon Hill
Designed by: Allan B. Calhamer
Year published: 1959
Number of players: 2–7
Grade level: High school

Double Shutter
Published by: Blue Orange Games
Designed by: Thierry Denoual
Year published: 2007
Number of players: 1–6
Grade levels: Elementary and
middle school

duck! duck! GO!
Published by: APE Games
Designed by: Kevin G. Nunn
Year published: 2008
Number of players: 2–6
Grade levels: Elementary and
middle school

El Grande
Published by: Rio Grande Games
and Hans im Glück
Designed by: Richard Ulrich and
Wolfgang Kramer
Year published: 1995
Number of players: 2–5
Grade level: High school

Enchanted Forest
Published by: Ravensburger
Designed by: Alex Randolph and
    Michel Matschoss
Year published: 1981
Number of players: 2–6
Grade level: Elementary school

España 1936
Published by: Devir
Designed by: Antonio Catalán
Year published: 2007
Number of players: 2
Grade level: High school

Formula D
Published by: Asmodée Editions
Designed by: Eric Randall and
    Laurent Lavaur
Year published: 2008
Number of players: 2–10
Grade levels: Middle and high
    school

Froggy Boogie
Published by: Blue Orange Games
Designed by: Thierry Denoual
Year published: 2007
Number of players: 2–6
Grade level: Elementary school

Ghost Stories
Published by: Asmodée Editions
    and Repos Production
Designed by: Antoine Bauza
Year published: 2008
Number of players: 2–6
Grade levels: Middle and high
    school

Gopher It!
Published by: Playroom
    Entertainment
Designed by: Reinhard Staupe
Year published: 2003

Number of players: 2–4
Grade level: Elementary school

Hamsterrolle
Published by: Zoch Verlag
Designed by: Jacques Zeimet
Year published: 2000
Number of players: 2–4
Grade levels: Middle and high
    school

Here I Stand
Published by: GMT Games
Designed by: Ed Beach
Year published: 2006
Number of players: 3–6
Grade level: High school

Hey! That's My Fish!
Published by: Mayfair Games and
    Phalanx Games
Designed by: Alvydas Jakeliunas
    and Günter Cornett
Year published: 2003
Number of players: 2–4
Grade level: Middle school

Hive
Published by: Gen Four Two
Designed by: John Yianni
Year published: 2001
Number of players: 2
Grade levels: Middle and high
    school

In the Country
Published by: HABA—Habermaaß
    GmbH
Designed by: Markus Nikisch
Year published: 2006
Number of players: 2–4
Grade level: Elementary school

Incan Gold
Published by: FRED Distribution

Designed by: Alan R. Moon and
Bruno Faidutti
Year published: 2006
Number of players: 3–8
Grade levels: Elementary and
middle school

LetterFlip
Published by: Out of the Box
Designed by: Ruddell Designs
Year published: 2004
Number of players: 2
Grade levels: Elementary and
middle school

Lord of the Rings
Published by: Fantasy Flight
Games
Designed by: Reiner Knizia
Year published: 2000
Number of players: 2–5
Grade levels: Middle and high
school

Lost Cities
Published by: Rio Grande Games
and Kosmos
Designed by: Reiner Knizia
Year published: 1999
Number of players: 2
Grade levels: Middle and high
school

M Is for Mouse
Published by: Playroom
Entertainment
Designed by: Reinhard Staupe
Year published: 2006
Number of Players: 2–5
Grade level: Elementary school

Manifest Destiny
Published by: GMT Games
Designed by: Bill Crenshaw

Year published: 2005
Number of players: 3–5
Grade level: High school

Max
Published by: Family Pastimes,
Ltd.
Designed by: Jim Deacove
Year published: 1986
Number of players: 1–8
Grade level: Elementary school

Memoir '44
Published by: Days of Wonder
Designed by: Richard Borg
Year published: 2004
Number of players: 2
Grade levels: Middle and high
school

My Word!
Published by: Out of the Box
Designed by: Reiner Knizia
Year published: 2001
Number of players: 2–6
Grade levels: Elementary and
middle school

Nanofictionary
Published by: Looney Labs
Designed by: Andrew Looney
Year published: 2002
Number of players: 3–6
Grade levels: Elementary and
middle school

**1960: The Making of
the President**
Published by: Z-Man Games, Inc.
Designed by: Christian Leonhard
and Jason Matthews
Year published: 2007
Number of players: 2
Grade level: High school

Number Chase

Published by: Playroom
  Entertainment
Designed by: Reinhard Staupe
Year published: 2006
Number of players: 2–5
Grade level: Elementary school

Numbers League

Published by: Bent Castle
  Workshops
Designed by: Chris Pallace and
  Ben Crenshaw
Year published: 2007
Number of players: 2–4
Grade levels: Elementary and
  middle school

Once upon a Time

Published by: Atlas Games
Designed by: Andrew Rilstone,
  James Wallis, and Richard
  Lambert
Year published: 1993
Number of players: 2–6
Grade levels: Middle and high
  school

Orchard

Published by: HABA—Habermaaß
  GmbH
Designed by: Anneliese
  Farkaschovsky
Year published: 1986
Number of players: 2–8
Grade level: Elementary school

Oregon

Published by: Rio Grande Games
  and Hans im Glück
Designed by: Henrik Berg and Ase
  Berg
Year published: 2007
Number of players: 2–4
Grade levels: Middle and high
  school

Pandemic

Published by: Z-Man Games,
  Inc.
Designed by: Matt Leacock
Year published: 2008
Number of players: 2–4
Grade levels: Middle and high
  school

Pillars of the Earth

Published by: Mayfair Games and
  Kosmos
Designed by: Michael Reineck and
  Stefan Stadler
Year published: 2006
Number of players: 2–4
Grade levels: Middle and high
  school

PitchCar

Published by: Ferti
Designed by: Jean du Poel
Year published: 1995
Number of players: 2–8
Grade levels: Middle and high
  school

Polarity

Published by: Ferti and Temple
  Games
Designed by: Douglas Seaton
Year published: 1986
Number of players: 2–4
Grade levels: Middle and high
  school

Portrayal

Published by: Braincog, Inc.
Designed by: Amanda Kohout and
  William Jacobson
Year published: 2006
Number of players: 3–10
Grade levels: Middle and high
  school

Power Grid
Published by: Rio Grande Games
and 2F Spiele
Designed by: Friedemann Friese
Year published: 2004
Number of players: 2–6
Grade levels: Middle and high
school

Prophecy
Published by: Z-Man Games, Inc.
Designed by: Vlaada (Vladimír)
Chvátil
Year published: 2002
Number of players: 2–5
Grade levels: Middle and high
school

Puerto Rico
Published by: Rio Grande Games
and Alea
Designed by: Andreas Seyfarth
Year published: 2002
Number of players: 3–5
Grade level: High school

Quiddler
Published by: Set Enterprises,
Inc.
Designed by: Marsha Falco
Year published: 1998
Number of players: 1–8
Grade levels: Elementary, middle,
and high school

Race for the Galaxy
Published by: Rio Grande Games
Designed by: Thomas Lehmann
Year published: 2007
Number of players: 2–4
Grade level: High school

RoboRally
Published by: Avalon Hill
Designed by: Richard Garfield

Year published: 1994
Number of players: 2–8
Grade levels: Middle and high
school

San Juan
Published by: Rio Grande Games
and Alea
Designed by: Andreas Seyfarth
Year published: 2004
Number of players: 2–4
Grade levels: Middle and high
school

Settlers of Catan
Published by: Mayfair Games
Designed by: Klaus Teuber
Year published: 1995
Number of players: 3–4
Grade levels: Middle and high
school

7 Ate 9
Published by: Out of the Box
Designed by: Maureen Hiron
Year published: 2009
Number of players: 2–4
Grade levels: Elementary and
middle school

Shadows over Camelot
Published by: Days of Wonder
Designed by: Serge Laget and
Bruno Cathala
Year published: 2005
Number of players: 3–7
Grade levels: Middle and high
school

Shiver-Stone Castle
Published by: HABA—Habermaaß
GmbH
Designed by: Kai Haferkamp and
Markus Nikisch
Year published: 2003

Number of players: 1–6
Grade level: Elementary school

Stone Age

Published by: Rio Grande Games
and Hans im Glück
Designed by: Bernd Brunnhofer
and Michael Tummelhofer
Year published: 2008
Number of players: 2–4
Grade levels: Middle and high
school

The Suitcase Detectives

Published by: HABA—Habermaaß
GmbH
Designed by: Guido Hoffmann
Year published: 2008
Number of players: 2–4
Grade level: Elementary school

Talisman

Published by: Fantasy Flight
Games
Designed by: John Goodenough
and Robert Harris
Year published: 2007
Number of players: 2–6
Grade levels: Middle and high
school

10 Days series (10 Days in Africa, 10 Days in Europe, 10 Days in Asia, 10 Days in the USA)

Published by: Out of the Box
Designed by: Aaron Weissblum
and Alan R. Moon
Year published: 2003
Number of players: 2–4
Grade levels: Elementary and
middle school

Through the Ages

Published by: FRED
Distribution

Designed by: Vlaada (Vladimír)
Chvátil
Year published: 2006
Number of players: 2–4
Grade level: High school

Ticket to Ride

Published by: Days of Wonder
Designed by: Alan R. Moon
Year published: 2004
Number of players: 2–5
Grade levels: Middle and high
school

Time's Up! Title Recall!

Published by: R and R Games
Designed by: Michael Adams and
Peter Sarrett
Year published: 2008
Number of players: 3–18
Grade levels: Middle and high
school

Tribune: Primus Inter Pares

Published by: Fantasy Flight Games
Designed by: Karl-Heinz Schmiel
Year published: 2007
Number of players: 2–5
Grade levels: Middle and high
school

Tumblin-Dice

Published by: Ferti and Nash Games
Designed by: Randy Nash
Year published: 2004
Number of players: 2–4
Grade levels: Elementary, middle,
and high school

24/7 the Game

Published by: Sunriver Games
Designed by: Carey Grayson
Year published: 2006
Number of players: 2–4
Grade level: Middle school

Twilight Struggle
Published by: GMT Games
Designed by: Ananda Gupta and
   Jason Matthews
Year published: 2005
Number of players: 2
Grade level: High school

Ultimate Werewolf:
Ultimate Edition
Published by: Bézier Games
Designed by: Ted Alspach
Year published: 2008
Number of players: 5–68
Grade levels: Middle and high
   school

VisualEyes
Published by: Buffalo Games, Inc.
Designed by: Keith Dugald and
   Steve Pickering
Year published: 2003
Number of players: 2–8
Grade levels: Elementary, middle,
   and high school

Werewolves of Miller's Hollow
Published by: Lui-Même and
   Amsodée Editions

Designed by: Dimitry Davidoff,
   Hervé Marly, and Philippe
   des Pallières
Year published: 2001
Number of players: 8–18
Grade levels: Middle and high
   school

Wits and Wagers
Published by: North Star Games,
   LLC
Designed by: Dominic
   Crapuchettes, Nate Heasley,
   and Satish Pillalamarri
Year published: 2005
Number of players: 3–7
Grade levels: Middle and high
   school

World of Warcraft: The
Adventure Game
Published by: Fantasy Flight
   Games
Designed by: Corey
   Konieczka
Year published: 2008
Number of players: 2–4
Grade level: High school

List of Game Publishers

Download this list from the Web: www.ala.org/editions/extras/mayer10092.

APE Games
E-mail: products@apegames.com
Website: www.apegames.com

Asmodée Editions
55 Avenue du Mont Royal West
Suite 207
Montreal, Quebec H2T 2S6
Canada
E-mail: contact_us@asmodee.com
Website: www.asmodee-us.com

Atlas Games
885 Pierce Butler Route
St. Paul, MN 55104
Phone: 651-638-0077
E-mail: info@atlas-games.com
Website: www.atlas-games.com

Avalon Hill
Wizards of the Coast
ATTN: Game Support
P.O. Box 707
Renton, WA 98057-0707
Phone: 800-324-6496
Website: www.wizards.com/
    default.asp?x=ah/welcome

Bent Castle Workshops
P.O. Box 10551
Rochester, NY 14610-0551
Phone: 540-731-0005
E-mail: knot@enchantedglyph.com
Website: www.bentcastle.com

Bézier Games
E-mail: ted@bezier.com
Website: http://games.bezier.com

Blue Orange Games
1000 Illinois Street
San Francisco, CA 94107
Phone: 415-252-0372
E-mail: info@blueorangegames.com
Website: www.blueorangegames.com

Braincog, Inc.
4702 Jamesville Drive
Matthews, NC 28105
Phone: 704-841-8522
E-mail: info@braincog.com
Website: www.braincog.com

Buffalo Games, Inc.
220 James E. Casey Drive
Buffalo, NY 14206
Phone: 800-832-2331
E-mail: bgames@buffalogames.com
Website: www.buffalogames.com

Days of Wonder
334 State Street
Suite 203
Los Altos, CA 94022
Website: www.daysofwonder.com/
en/

Devir US LLC
309 S. Cloverdale Street
Seattle, WA 98108
Phone: 206-764-9499
Toll free: 877-DEVIR50
E-mail: questions@devir.pt
Website: www.devir.us

Family Pastimes, Ltd.
RR 4
Perth, Ontario K7H 3C6
Canada
Phone: 613-267-4819
E-mail: info@familypastimes.com
Website: www.familypastimes.com

Fantasy Flight Games
1975 W. County Road B2
Roseville, MN 55113
Phone: 651-639-1905
Website: www.fantasyflightgames
.com

Ferti
ZI du Phare
27 rue François Arago
33700 Mérignac
France
E-mail: contact@ferti-games.com
Website: http://ferti.free.fr/index-e
.php

FRED Distribution
Keith Blume
Managing Director
Phone: 773-684-2633
E-mail: keithblume@gmail.com
Website: www.freddistribution.com

Gen42 Games
Website: www.genfourtwo.com

GMT Games
P.O. Box 1308
Hanford, CA 93232
Phone: 800-523-6111
E-mail: gmtoffice@gmtgames.com
Website: www.gmtgames.com

HABA USA
4407 Jordan Road
P.O. Box 42
Skaneateles, NY 13152-9371
Phone: 800-468-6873
Website: www.habausa.com

Looney Labs
P.O. Box 761
College Park, MD 20741
Phone: 301-441-1019
Fax: 301-441-4871
E-mail: thelab@looneylabs.com
Website: www.looneylabs.com

Mayfair Games
8060 St. Louis Avenue
Skokie, IL 60076
Phone: 847-677-6655
E-mail: mayfair@mayfairgames
.com
Website: www.mayfairgames.com

North Star Games, LLC
5906 Jarvis Lane
Bethesda, MD 20814
Phone: 301-493-4331
E-mail: CustomerSupport@
NorthStarGames.com
Website: www.northstargames.com

Out of the Box
609 Bennett Road
Dodgeville, WI 53533
Phone: 800-540-2304
E-mail: info@otb-games.com
Website: www.otb-games.com

Playroom Entertainment
13236 Raymer Street
North Hollywood, CA 91605
Phone: 818-432-1112
Website: www.playrooment.com

R and R Games, Inc.
P.O. Box 130195
Tampa, FL 33629
Phone: 888-8RIDDLE
Website: www.rnrgames.com

Ravensburger USA
1 Puzzle Lane
Newton, NH 03858
Phone: 603-257-1500
Website: www.ravensburger.com/
    usa/home/index.html

Rio Grande Games
P.O. Box 45715
Rio Rancho, NM 87174
Website: www.riograndegames
    .com

Set Enterprises, Inc.
16537 E. Laser Drive
Suite 6
Fountain Hills, AZ 85268
E-mail: setgame@setgame.com
Website: www.setgame.com

Sunriver Games LLC
16548 SW Willow Drive
Sherwood, OR 97140
E-mail: info@sunrivergames.com
Website: www.sunrivergames.com

Warfrog Games
E-mail: martin@warfroggames.com
Website: www.warfroggames.com

Z-Man Games, Inc.
6 Alan Drive
Mahopac, NY 10541
Phone: 845-208-3502
E-mail: zman@zmangames.com
Website: www.zmangames.com

Zoch Verlag
Brienner Str. 54a
80333 München
Germany
E-mail: info@zoch-verlag.com
Website: www.zoch-verlag.com/
    en.html

Index

You may also be interested in

Serving Boys through Readers' Advisory: Based on more than twenty years' experience working to get boys interested in reading, Michael Sullivan now offers his first readers' advisory volume. With an emphasis on nonfiction and the boy-friendly categories of genre fiction, the work offers hundreds of suggested titles, booktalks, and lists to help turn boys into rabid readers.

Hosting a Library Mystery: Whether they're solving the morning crossword puzzle, working out whodunit in a best-selling thriller, or participating in the library's mystery book club, everyone loves a mystery! In *Hosting a Library Mystery*, Elizabeth Karle capitalizes on our delight in the genre with this unique, interactive programming guide.

New on the Job: From job search strategies and discovering your work philosophy to the nitty-gritty details of creating acceptable use policies, this resource serves as a wise mentor for new school library media specialists. Ruth Toor and Hilda K. Weisburg share the joys and perils of the profession along with a wealth of practical advice from a combined six decades of experience in library media centers and as collaborators on books, presentations, and workshops.

Protecting Intellectual Freedom in Your School Library: Tailored to the school library, this title presents a number of scenarios in which intellectual freedom is at risk and includes case studies that provide narrative treatment of common situations arising in school libraries; motivating ways to prepare new hires for handling intellectual freedom issues; sidebars throughout the book that offer sample policies, definitions of key terms, and analysis of important statutes and decisions; and detailed information on how to handle challenges to materials in your collection.

Order today at www.alastore.ala.org or 866-746-7252!